A SHORT HISTORY OF

SUNNINGDALE

SUNNINGDALE CHURCH, 1864

Photo: R.W. End

A SHORT HISTORY OF
SUNNINGDALE

WITH SOME NOTES ON WENTWORTH

BY

F.C. HODDER

FOREWORD
BY
R.S. BREWIS

FURTHER FOREWORD
BY
B.B. WADE

TAKAHE PUBLISHING LTD.
2011

This edition published 2011 by:
Takahe Publishing Ltd.
Registered Office:
77 Earlsdon Street, Coventry, CV5 6EL

Copyright © Takahe Publishing Ltd. 2011

All rights reserved. This publication may not be reproduced, stored in a retrieval system or transmitted, in any form or by any means, electronic, mechanical, photocopying, recording or otherwise, without the prior permission of the publishers.

FOREWORD

ALTHOUGH Mr. Hodder's purpose was primarily to write a history of Sunningdale, he has traversed so many districts and touched on such divers topics that this book should be welcomed by a much wider circle than the title would suggest: Wentworth, Chobham, Old Windsor, Fort Belvedere, Virginia Water, Chertsey Abbey, and many other interesting places are so closely connected with Sunningdale that they inevitably form part of its history.

Much of antiquarian interest is included in the earlier part of the book.

From earliest days the main highway to the West appears to have passed through Sunningdale. Situated near the junction of two Roman roads in the midst of wild forest and bog, Sunningdale groped its way through the middle ages; conflicting with the opulent monasticism of Chertsey Abbey was the genuine poverty of Broom Hall Nunnery; slowly the district has developed into what is to-day one of the most beautiful and sought after gardens of England.

Always the Road has played an important part. Many a highwayman's name is associated with the district, not the least romantic being that of Claude Duval, who trod a stately measure with his fair victim beneath the light of the moon. Lying alone among these wild wastes between Staines and Bagshot, Broom Hall Nunnery must have been a veritable haven of refuge to the traveller in the Middle Ages.

Throughout many reigns, numerous Princes have contrived to pass much of their leisure in and around the Forest of Windsor; many princely homes testify to their appreciation of the natural beauty of the neighbourhood. What was once the undisputed domain of the Hart Royal and the wild boar has now become the dormitory of the London business man, and the "Mecca" of golf champions.

The story of this evolution makes pleasant reading within these pages, and may provide some solution to the anomalies caused by the meeting and overlapping of so many civil and ecclesiastical parishes, counties, and postal districts.

One may sometimes wonder what common interest one has with one's neighbour - here at any rate is another interest you can share.

The author must have taken unstinted trouble to have found so many links with the past that might otherwise have been lost, and has told the story so entertainingly and lucidly that I have no doubt it will be welcomed by every home in the district.

R. S. BREWIS.

FURTHER FOREWORD

Why republish a book written in 1936 when other, more up-to-date histories of the area are in circulation and when the author himself claims in his preface "there is no merit in this little volume"?

The author was too modest. F.C. Hodder was my grandfather and ever since I came to live in the house in which he ran Sunningdale Post Office, and which still carries his name above the "shop" window, people have been asking me if it was still possible to obtain copies of "A Short History of Sunningdale."

This book, referred to directly or indirectly in most of the articles and books that have been published in recent times, is a captivating blend of historical research, local knowledge and personal reminiscences. It is this personal involvement in the life and stories of this village and surrounding area, written by a man whose parents were married in Sunningdale Church in 1856, who grew up and spent his whole life in the village, that makes this book so much more than local history research.

By the time the book was written, the little village of only a few houses and cottages had grown and changed, yet as one turns the pages, one has the impression of being in a village where everyone is known by name. I wonder what my grandfather would make of the huge changes in character and in size of the Sunningdale he knew as a boy! And yet many of the houses and families he mentions are still part of the village; being designated "green belt" thankfully protects the remaining farmland and much of the old village has been declared a conservation area.

It is probably this awareness of living in a village which is under threat of losing its identity to the developers that has renewed the interest in this unique book. Those who have grown up in Sunningdale, or who have lived many years in this friendly and attractive village will, I am sure, be delighted to find this old 'friend' available again. Newcomers to the area will enjoy getting to know their neighbourhood better and find interest and pride in the history of the village they have chosen as their home.

I should like to end with a tribute to the

author. He writes in his preface that the origin of the book was a series of articles he had written in response to requests from the people of Sunningdale. In writing the articles, he had drawn on the store of information he had been collecting for between thirty and forty years. This he describes as a hobby. I know from the many papers in my possession, that another major hobby of his was writing; it is clear that here was a man who just could not stop putting pen to paper. Yet this was not the hobby of an otherwise idle man: he ran Sunningdale Post Office, brought up nine children, made beautifully carved items of furniture for his adored wife, collected a large library, had a small printing press in his shed and a dark room for developing his photographs. During the first world war, his postmen having enlisted as soldiers, he kept the mail deliveries going by employing men too sick to fight which meant that in bad weather they too were unavailable for duty. Being a man who put duty and consideration for others first, my grandfather would take the letters himself at the end of his busy day. His own health was never robust but customers for him were people and not numbers. I am convinced that this combination of caring about people and the place where they lived gave him the energy to complete his interest in local history by writing the articles which gave birth to this book.

I should like to thank the people of Sunningdale who have shown so much interest in the book and to Steven Hodder who has put in many hours of hard work to make the whole reprinting project a possibility.

B. B. WADE

To the inhabitants of Sunningdale, past, present and future, this little book is dedicated

CONTENTS

Chapter

I	Sunningdale	1
II	Stone and Bronze Ages	8
III	Roman Road	14
IV	Ancient Monument ..	36
V	Coworth	46
VI	Broomhall Nunnery ..	59
VII	Portnall Park, Wentworth, and the London Road ..	98
VIII	Our Church	113
IX	Our Schools	122
X	Parochial Charities ..	131
XI	Sunningdale and the Royal Family	141

PREFACE

THERE is no merit in this little volume, except, perhaps, the fact that it is, so far as I am aware, the first crude attempt to collect under one cover scraps of information gleaned from numerous books and other sources, with perhaps a few odds and ends picked up during the long period in which my family have been connected with Sunningdale.

I should never have ventured to publish this book, but for the fact that many readers of the Parish Magazine, in which most of this little history was first printed as a series of short articles, have expressed a wish to see it in book form. The origin of these articles is rather curious. I had been collecting all the information about Sunningdale that had come in my way for some thirty or forty years, not with an idea of publishing, but simply as a hobby, when, at a Parish Council meeting, some question arose as to the proceeds of the investment of the fund realised from the sale of the old gravel pit, and to my astonishment no one present knew where this gravel pit had been. Several guesses very wide of the mark were hazarded, and I then explained its situation. Thinking it over afterwards, I thought it might interest other people to know that the church was built on the site of this old pit, and might help in any future discussion that might arise if I wrote an account of it for the Parish Magazine, quoting the title deeds to show the exact position of the site. Upon its publication quite a number of people asked me if I would give some more historical notes of the village, and so I embarked upon a series of short articles, which seemed to be quite popular, and to arouse an interest much more widely spread than I had anticipated.

Strange to say, just after I had started these articles, the W.E.A. commenced a series of lectures on the subject of "Local History." The lecturer was Mr. Coles of Reading, who was most enthusiastic and energetic, and who introduced me to his friend Mr. Smallcombe, the curator of Reading Museum, and both these gentlemen have very kindly given me a great deal of help.

Mr. R. W. End has most kindly furnished me with photographs for the illustrations; Mrs. Fox, a granddaughter of John Alves Arbuthnot, Esq., who was for many years the owner of Coworth Park, very kindly examined and corrected my manuscript relating to that estate; Mrs. Fradgley gave me some additional facts concerning Broom Hall, and I owe much to several books, too numerous to mention individually, but I would like especially to speak of Mr. Hughes's "Windsor Forest," Mr. Turner's "History of Egham," the Berks and Bucks Archaeological Journals, which have been most helpful, and the *Windsor and Eton Express* from which I have gleaned much of recent events.

Sunningdale, October, 1936.

CHAPTER I

SUNNINGDALE

SITUATED as it is between Windsor Great Park on the one hand and Chobham Common on the other, there are few more delightful villages in the county of Berks than was the Sunningdale of my youthful days.

Since then many changes have taken place, some, no doubt improvements, but, alas! many, especially some of the more recent ones, to say the least, doubtful.

The whole of the civil parish of Sunningdale is in the county of Berkshire, and until 1895 formed a part of Old Windsor, some six or seven miles away, but the ecclesiastical parish, which was formed in 1840, includes portions of the parishes of Egham, Chobham, and Windlesham in Surrey, and perhaps that part of Sunningdale is better known to casual visitors than Sunningdale itself, as it is there that the well-known and extensive golf links stretch for miles over land that a few years ago was open common, covered with heather; the undisturbed home of the fox, the badger, the rabbit, the hare, and innumerable wild birds, some of them rarely seen near the haunts of men, which the advent of bricks and mortar of the last fifty years have unfortunately frightened into seeking new quarters.

Much of Sunningdale, with the exception of Coworth, originally formed part of Windsor Forest, which formerly extended for many more miles than it does now - in fact from Windsor right down to Basingstoke. The term "forest" in those days did not necessarily imply an area covered with trees, as we now understand it, but was also used to denote waste land, covered with heather or other undergrowth. As a matter of fact this district was almost treeless, except perhaps for a few sturdy oaks, which had managed to grow up in spite of innumerable deer, wild pigs and other animals, which browsed off the young shoots as soon as they appeared above ground. So rare were trees and shrubs that where they did exist, the places where they grew were named after them.

But to return to the Sunningdale of my youthful days. There were few houses here then. The church was small, and consisted of a nave and a square tower about forty feet high, the base of which formed an entrance porch above which there was a small gallery. A small chancel and side chapel had been added to the original structure by the Rev. W. C. Raffles Flint in 1860, as a memorial to his uncle, Sir Stamford Raffles, a former governor of the Straits Settlements, and one of the founders of the Zoological Gardens at Regent's Park. The nave was plastered inside and painted a deep cream colour, with one or two mural tablets on the walls. The outside was thickly covered with ivy. There was a small organ, which had been given by Mr. Arbuthnot, and the organ chamber served as a vestry. One could hardly describe the edifice as beautiful, but it was adequate for the people of those days. By 1887, however, the population had so increased that it was pulled down and the present church erected.

Of the larger houses the principal were: the Vicarage, occupied by the Rev. W. C. Raffles Flint; Sunningdale Park, by Sir Charles Crossley; Coworth Park, by John Alves Arbuthnot, Esq.; Lynwood, by Viscount Hood; Charters, by Edward Hamilton, Esq.; King's Beeches, by E. Barnett, Esq.; Rosemount, by G. Grogan,

Esq.; Wardour Lodge, by Captain Dallas; Park Lodge, by Sir David Wood; Broom Hall, by John Bulpit, Esq.; Broomfield Hall, by James Reiss, Esq.; Shrubs Hill Place, by John Torry, Esq.; Shrubs Hill House, by Dr. Chambers; The Nutshell, by the Misses Hardinge. Portnall Park, which, although not in Sunningdale, has for centuries been intimately connected with this village, was the seat of the Rev. H. J. Fane De Salis.

The cottages were not numerous, and many of them have been pulled down and more modern ones erected, with the addition of a great number of new ones on former fields, meadows, or wastes.

Sloping down the hill above the station were a couple of fields belonging to Broomhall Farm, but all beyond the brow of the first slope was open common, thick with heather and a few stunted pine trees; beyond that, towards Bagshot, was a great expanse of heather and gorse, with a small clearing and farm-house, officially designated "Broomhall Waste," but perhaps more graphically described by its local name of "Starveall Farm."

Near the station the only houses were the Station Hotel and Oak Lodge, the residence of the curate, the Rev. I. Wreford, and the old thatched cottage at the corner, now pulled down, which had formerly served as a residence for the turnpike gate keeper. On the other side of Broomhall Lane were the Chequers Inn, another old thatched cottage, and also a cottage near to Dagwell House.

Passing up the Chobham Road we came to Dagwell House, occupied by Mr. Joseph Norris, and his builder's yard and workshops adjoining, then three or four cottages and the brickfields, with a brick kiln and a few more cottages connected with the brick works, and then the open common, with Titlark's Farm cut out of it. One could go for miles over the heath without meeting a soul, unless the common had troops encamped upon it or carrying out manoeuvres, as frequently happened in the summer months. What a glorious place it was for a picnic; what a refuge for birds, rabbits, and hares! And what a place for gipsy encampments!

Turning to another part of the district, the Rise, consisting of over eighty houses, is built on what was at that time a rather swampy field. Wilbury, Littleridge, and Ferndale occupy what was the site of a thick belt of pines, Sunningdale School, Charters Road, and the surrounding houses are on what was rough heath land with some belts of pine trees, and the playing fields at Sunningdale School have replaced brickyards. A part of King's Beech Hill Road was absorbed into Sunningdale Park before my time, and another portion into the grounds of Sunningdale School about fifty years ago or less.

Such are some of the changes that have taken place - changes obliterating old landmarks, and greater perhaps than those of many centuries previously.

Another and more recent change is the destruction of Broomfield Hall and its beautiful grounds for the erection of villas and flats. For the same cause, Scotswood was broken up some years ago, but in the case of that estate the mansion was left standing and was converted into flats.

THE SUNNINGDALE URNS
Bronze Age

CHAPTER II

THE STONE AND BRONZE AGES

TO the casual observer it may appear strange that we have little or no evidence of Palaeolithic or Neolithic man in Sunningdale, for on the face of it it would seem that the conditions here would have been ideal from the point of view of prehistoric man. The country generally was open heather, teeming with game such as he coveted. Dangerous wild beasts, with which his primitive stone and bone weapons were inadequate to cope, confined themselves almost entirely to the distant woods and forests, and if they did venture into the open heathlands during the day, could be clearly detected from such a distance as made it easily possible to avoid them. But in spite of this the only Stone Age implement, so far as I know, that has ever been discovered in the immediate neighbourhood, is a stone hammer head which was found at Sunninghill some years ago.

If, however, we consider the matter for a few moments, we shall see the reason why this district was unpopulated. Flint weapons were delicate instruments and very easily broken, consequently they had constantly to be replaced. In our sandy soil there is little or no flint - certainly none of any size such as would be required for spears and knives. Such flints are almost always found in layers more or less thick in the chalk deposits, and so primitive man would not be likely to venture very far from where the materials for such fragile instruments could be found and his broken weapons easily replaced, unless driven by starvation or some equally powerful incentive.

But with the coming of the Bronze Age conditions were entirely altered. Man had now a material which did not easily break, and his weapons, by means of a piece of sandstone, which he could always carry about with him, could easily be sharpened when the edge became dull. He could, therefore, wander much further afield without fear of being stranded without the means of defence from wild beasts, or of attacking the game which he so much desired. So this neighbourhood became more or less populated, and judging from the evidence afforded by the number of barrows which have been located in the district, the hunting grounds round here must have been popular.

Most of the barrows are on high ground, and one of them near Sunningdale station was opened in 1901, under the supervision of Mr. A. A. Shrubsole, F.G.S., and Mr. Colyer of the Reading Museum. Mr. Shrubsole subsequently read a paper with reference to this and other barrows found in Berkshire before the Society of Antiquaries, a copy of which was kindly lent to me by Mr. Coles, and from which I have gained the following particulars.

In this barrow were found no less than 23 cinerary urns and two deposits of cremated remains without urns. Though all the urns were more or less broken, it was possible to see that some of them were of very large size - one, I believe, was the largest ever found in this country. They were of earthenware, some fairly well baked, and others imperfectly baked, and were probably made from the deposits of clay near the foot of the hill, which were until a few years ago worked as brickfields. All appear to have had some primitive form of ornament, a band or fillet of clay about an inch wide running round the urn about three and a half inches from the top, impressed with the top of a finger at short intervals. It is rather interesting to note that in many cases the print of a finger-nail is clearly shown. The finger must have been that of a girl or woman, as the impressions are too small for those of a man. This would seem to indicate that the potter's work was done by the women. As a matter of fact, it is pretty certain that most of the manual work would be done by the women, as the men would be fully occupied in making their weapons, hunting food, fighting wild beasts, and protecting their homes from marauding tribes.

In one of the urns was found a piece of a broken cooking-pot, and in another a piece of flint, evidently such as was used for kindling fire.

Unfortunately much of the collection was dispersed, even before it had been properly examined, but several pieces were preserved and presented by Mr. Roberts to the Reading Museum, where they now are.

There are still two other smaller tumuli,

which could not be opened owing to their being right on the golf course, but as they are in a good state of preservation it is to be hoped that they will be taken care of, and perhaps at some future time there may be an opportunity of opening and investigating them.

In the tumulus opened, it is significant to note that nearly all the interments were on the south and south-west, which would seem to indicate that the deceased were sun worshippers. More than half of the urns were in an inverted position. This was by no means unusual, and various conjectures as to the reason for so placing cinerary urns have been brought forward from time to time. The most favoured seems to be the fear that the spirits of the dead might return to haunt the living, and one may readily understand that people holding such a belief would fear the spirits of some people more than those of others, so that when some particularly unpleasant individual was disposed of, they would take what they hoped were precautions to make his return as difficult as possible.

In many cases tumuli were formed with

beautifully smoothed floors, of chalk or silver sand, all made as comfortable as possible, and the urns placed on them, either in an upright position, when they were covered with a stone slab, or inverted, as the case might be, and the whole then covered with a layer of sharp flints, or rough stones, apparently with the object of making it as difficult and unpleasant as possible for the spirits of the dead to return.

It is rather significant to note that in every case primitive and heathen people have religious rites of some sort, showing that man must worship something, and no matter what form their religion may take - and some of the forms are most horrible - there is always a belief in the immortality of the soul.

CHAPTER III

THE ROMAN ROAD

PERHAPS the most interesting relic of the past we have in Sunningdale is the Roman Road, a wonderful piece of engineering, of so stupendous a character that the Saxons when they saw it could not believe that it was the work of men, and so christened it "The Devil's Highway." Perhaps that was the reason why they did not make use of it, but allowed it to lie derelict, so that it eventually became overgrown and nearly all trace of it lost for centuries.

When I was a schoolboy, in some way I got the impression that the Britons, before the Roman invasion, were a race of barbarians, who painted themselves with woad, wore undressed skins of animals for clothing, and had no knowledge of any of the arts until the introduction of Roman civilisation. I think this must have been the fault of the text books we used in those days, which were dry and uninteresting, and not calculated to give the young any idea of how fascinating the study of history can be. They also somehow conveyed the idea that the invasions of 55 and 54 B.C. settled the Roman occupation of Britain, but gave no information, so far as I can remember, that there was a break of no less than 97 years between the second invasion of Julius Caesar and the more complete occupation from A.D. 43.

Actually, the Britons had attained quite a high degree of civilisation before even the first invasion of the Romans. They wore clothing made from a rough sort of cloth woven on hand looms; they had mastered the art of making tools and ornaments of bronze; they were quite good workers in wood, and had even discovered the use of the lathe. They used wheeled carts, and had so developed them that the wheels were made with spokes, hubs, and felloes as they are today, instead of the solid wheels at first used. Their chariots were superior - at any rate for use in this country as it then was - to the Roman ones. In fact, I am quite prepared to believe that in some respects they were even in advance of their conquerors.

Their weak point was that, consisting of several nations as they did, they could never for any length of time work together without jealousy and distrust, so when they banded together to meet the common enemy, although they had weapons, chariots, and generals in no way inferior to those of the Romans, and had very ingeniously constructed strong fortresses of earth and timber, this weakness did more than anything to cause their defeat.

Coway Stakes, near Walton-on-Thames, took its name from a most ingenious and formidable arrangement of sharpened piles shod with lead and driven into the river bed, which the Romans found it most difficult to overcome, and had the barrier been defended by a really united body of troops, they would probably never have crossed the river.

When Julius Caesar finally left Britain in the autumn of 54 B.C. he may have left some of his troops, or more probably some civilians, behind, and during the long period of 97 years which followed, Roman ideas and practices gradually percolated through the southern parts of Britain, so that when the Romans came again in A.D. 43, more or less by invitation, they found a country already partially Romanised, and prepared to accept the manners and customs of the great Empire.

Recognising the vital importance of safe and quick communications, one of the first acts performed by the Romans in the countries they occupied was to construct complete systems of roads, and so skilful had they become in the art of road building that even with the advance in knowledge and science of later years we could probably teach them nothing in this way - unless it is the use of tar - and until Macadam again introduced scientifically constructed roads they were far superior to any made in this country after they had left it.

These splendid roads formed a complete network throughout England and enabled the Romans in case of necessity to convey large bodies of troops and supplies with ease and rapidity from any of the garrisons to points of danger.

Of course all this took time, and it must have been many years before the whole system was complete, but I am inclined to think that the road we are immediately concerned with was perhaps one of the earliest made, as it linked up several important points. It started from Londinium (London) and coming by way of Oxford Street, Tyburn (Hyde Park),

Turnham Green, and Hounslow, it reached the river Thames at a point near Staines named by the Romans "Pontes." The point where it crossed the river is not exactly known, nor has the site of the place called Pontes been definitely fixed. Some say that it was a point between the bridge carrying the railway and the one carrying the road at Staines, but I am rather inclined to think that it was a little higher up and that the bridges were over the Colne and the Thames, thus accounting for the plural. Probably the river has changed its course since then, and become narrower and deeper. Most likely at some time the whole of Runnymede was a shallow lake with the river meandering through it, or at any rate a large swamp subject to periodical floodings. This seems to be indicated by the construction at a much later date of the causeway between Egham and Staines.

I think it highly probable that the town of Pontes was on the hill at Englefield Green overlooking the river, as this would be a much healthier spot for a permanent camp for troops than the low-lying swampy ground close to the river bank, and yet would be close enough for the complete protection of the bridges in case of a threatened assault. From time to time traces of Roman remains have been found which would indicate the existence of a settlement there, although I believe no thorough investigation has ever been made.

The road runs in a perfectly straight line from Bakeham House to Rapley Farm at Duke's Hill near Bagshot. Traces of it were found when Virginia Water was made, and when l was a boy, its course through the grounds of Belvedere Fort was plainly visible after a shower of rain, when the line of the road dried up much more rapidly than the surrounding ground, presumably because it was better drained owing to the Roman method of construction.

From the Belvedere it passed through Coworth to a point near to the gate to the path through the church fields, through the grounds of Wardour Lodge, through Charters Pond Clump and almost following the course of Gravel Hill Road, near to the Fireball Clump, and through the Belt to Charters Pond, and so across to Rapley Farm, where one of the fields now called Roman Down must have been the site of a settlement of some importance as many Roman remains have been found there. Here the road forked, one branch going to Silchester, the Roman Calleva Atrebatum, and the other to Winchester (Venta Belgarum) and Chichester (Regnum).

Rapley Farm must have been an important station, for it was not only the junction of the Winchester and Silchester roads, but from it was a road to the important fortress at St. George's Hill, Weybridge, and so through to Wimbledon. This road passed through Chobham Common about a mile south of the encampment at Sunningdale.

But to return to the road with which we are more concerned - the one to Silchester - at Rapley Farm it turned westward at an angle 25 degrees from its former course, and the next point of interest reached is Wickham Bushes, where the many remains show that there must have been a very considerable settlement, consisting of wooden houses, as shown by the great number of nails which have been unearthed, and probably also some of wattle and daub. Here were found portions of pottery, coins and other relics. Passing on, we come to the junction of a short road to Caesar's Camp at Easthampstead, a place which it is very unlikely that Caesar ever saw, which lies about half a mile to the north of the road to Silchester. This extensive encampment was evidently a British stronghold adopted by the Romans for their own use, and considerably strengthened by them. It is shaped much like an oak leaf, and, according to Roman usage, would probably accommodate nine thousand men. When occupied by the Romans it must have been a very strong place indeed. On the northern side, where the ground slopes steeply away, there was a wide ditch and a high embankment; on the other sides, where the approach is more gentle, a ditch and double embankment.

Before the coming of the Romans this enclosure may have been used for the protection of cattle or sheep in time of danger. The objection to this theory is that the surrounding country is mostly barren heathland and not suitable for grazing, but this may be due to climatic and other changes, and although undoubtedly the land was always poor, it may have provided good grazing a couple of thousand years ago. Such climatic changes occurred in Europe and

Asia during the Bronze Age, causing the migration of whole tribes, and indeed were still going on while the Romans were in Britain, and ultimately caused the fall of the Roman Empire.

Returning to the main road, we come to Silchester, the Calleva Atrebatum of the Romans. This place is on a plateau about a mile and a half from the present village of Silchester, and is mainly in the grounds of Strathfieldsaye. The Duke of Wellington very kindly allowed it to be excavated and thoroughly explored, a work which occupied some sixteen years. It covered an area of 102 acres, and the excavations have given us much insight into the manners and customs of the Romans in Britain, as well as revealing their methods of building towns and fortifications. Unfortunately the Amphitheatre, which lies on a neighbouring property, has not been explored, as the owner would not give permission for excavation, but it is to be hoped that some day this may be as thoroughly examined as was the rest of the city.

A fine bronze Roman Eagle, which was undoubtedly the finial of the staff of a standard, was taken to Strathfieldsaye, where it is preserved, and the Reading Museum has been enriched with the finest collection of Roman remains in the south of England.

Before it was occupied by the Romans Silchester must have been an important stronghold of the Britons. It appears first to have been occupied by the Segontiaci; a stone was found in 1732 bearing the inscription "Deo Herculi Saegontiacorum," which suggests this. They appear to have been driven out by the Atrebates, a tribe from the neighbourhood of Arras in Gaul, who in turn were dispossessed by the Romans, who made it an almost impregnable city. Around it was a deep ditch or moat, then came walls eight feet thick and about twenty feet high, and inside this an embankment nearly or quite as high as the walls. There were seven gates from which roads radiated.

From the eastern gate ran the road of which we have been speaking. From another a road through Basingstoke to Winchester (Venta Belgarum) and thence to Chichester (Regnum) and Bittern on Southampton Water; another to Old Sarum

(Sorbiodumium) by what is called the Port Way; one to Bath (Aquae Sulis) by way of Speen (Spinae); one to the north to Streatley and Dorchester; a sixth by way of Reading to Bray; and one from the southern gate to Vindomis, a place near Lower Froyle.

And now a word or two about the city itself may not be amiss, although perhaps it is somewhat outside the scope of this book, which was originally intended only to deal with the Roman Road as it concerns Sunningdale, yet, to understand thoroughly its significance and the great amount of traffic it must have carried, it is well to consider the importance of the place it served.

Silchester, then, was a centre in which, as I have already said, several roads leading to large towns in the south and west met, and it was probably a great clearing station. Aquae Sulis was a very important city, and itself a centre from which the roads of the west radiated, yet it must have been much inferior in size and importance to Silchester. All the traffic from east to west and vice versa, and from London to the south must have passed along our road, making it an exceedingly busy one - even although there were no motor-cars or buses!

In Silchester itself there was a large Forum, a Basilica and an Amphitheatre. The houses were of two types, courtyard and corridor, and each stood in its own grounds, surrounded by garden and lawns. They were mostly tiled or thatched, but some were covered with thin slabs of stone. The tiles were large and thick, and at each side had a ridge or fillet formed on them about an inch high. They were laid side by side, and a sort of ridge tile placed over the adjacent fillets to render them waterproof. When stone was used as a covering it was cut into thin slabs and the pieces overlapped like fish scales, very much as slates are used to-day.

The windows, which, from the fact that they were placed high up in the walls, were evidently intended only for letting in light and not for seeing through, were glazed with glass of a greenish colour, somewhat obscured or frosted inside and smooth outside. These windows illustrate the phrase "Now we see through a glass darkly, etc." This glass was evidently cast to shape and size and not cut, and was generally fixed with fillets across the corners, although in some cases traces of a cement for securing the panes were found. The walls were usually colour washed, yellow, red, blue, or green, or some other bright colour. The poorer houses usually had ordinary tiled floors, but the better ones had very beautiful mosaics.

The Romans seem not to have liked our cold winters, for the houses appear all to have had a system of central heating, known as the hypocaust. It consisted of small rooms or cellars about three feet high under the floors, which were supported by pillars. These low rooms were heated by charcoal furnaces fed from outside, and from them hollow pillars or pilasters conveyed the hot air to moulded tiles forming channels round the rooms. In houses with a second storey the pipes were carried on round the upper rooms as well as the lower.

The public baths were a very important institution in a Roman city, and there were very large ones at Silchester. A Roman exquisite would sometimes spend half the day in them, and probably much of the news circulated there - and no doubt a certain amount of scandal. The bathers went first into rooms where they were made to sweat freely, then into a very hot bath, after which they were scraped down with a piece of bronze shaped much like a modern curry-comb, they then lounged about in a tepid room and from there passed into a room still cooler and then into a frigid area where they had a cold bath and an attendant rubbed them down with olive oil. In a room of one of the baths were found remains of artistic and beautifully made bottles which had contained scents and oils.

Very few lamps have been found, but a great many candlesticks, which seems to indicate that candles were the usual means of illumination.

Large potteries must have existed in the neighbourhood, and have in fact been recently discovered, for much pottery, some perfect, but most of it more or less broken, was found. But the pottery was not all made locally, for there was much beautiful Samian ware, which was evidently imported from the neighbourhood of Marseilles, and there was also a quantity of black Upchurch ware.

The water supply was obtained from wells, a number of which have been found. Most of them were square and lined with timber, but in one case wine barrels were used for lining a round well. These barrels are now in the Museum.

Few animal bones were discovered in the rubbish heaps, but this may be accounted for by the fact that there was a large industry carried on in bone carving. Another industry was dyeing. Wool was brought in from the Downs and manufactured into cloth and dyed various beautiful colours.

There were some small heaps of coins, probably the hoards of slaves, as they were mostly copper or bronze and of little value. One lot, however, contained about 250 silver coins. The Romans had attained such a degree of excellency in the minting of coins that it is only within the last two hundred and fifty years that we have been able to produce their equal. The coins ranged over a long period - from 39 B.C. to the last Emperor, Honorius, A.D. 410, One coin of Augustus was found.

There were no remains of fireplaces or

ovens. It is believed that the Romans usually cooked meat on grids or before the fire, but they also possessed portable ovens.

Some surgical instruments of a kind which indicate that the Romans must have had a good knowledge of surgery were discovered. Another discovery was a very perfect seal of Nero in an excellent state of preservation. Other interesting objects were a pocket knife very similar to those in use to-day, tiles with the footprints of a deer and fawn chased by a wolf deeply impressed in the clay before baking, and on another scratched by some lovesick Roman potter the word "puellam" telling us of the old, old, ever new story, popular then as now. Many of the tiles have short inscriptions or names scratched on them by a pointed stick when the clay was soft, probably by youthful workmen who were proud of their handiwork. Some were marked by the footprints of birds, and small animals and finger-prints are not uncommon, but perhaps the most interesting is the clear imprint of the bare foot of a small child.

In a workshop was an iron plane such as is used to-day, yet the plane was only reinvented in the latter part of the seventeenth or the beginning of the eighteenth century!

Only one human skeleton was unearthed. It had apparently been buried under a floor. Was this evidence of an undetected crime committed more than fifteen hundred years ago?

Recently the cemetery belonging to Silchester has been discovered, but I think has not yet been thoroughly explored. Investigation, if undertaken, may give some interesting results.

The city contained not only temples to the Roman gods, but also a Christian church, which shows that the Romans must have been quite tolerant people.

Did St. Paul ever preach in Silchester? I think it may have been possible, although apparently the church was not built until much later than his time. Calleva was undoubtedly one of the earliest towns occupied by the Romans, and if St. Paul really visited his friends in Chichester, as many think he did, it is very unlikely that he would have left Britain without visiting

Calleva Atrebatum, which must have been quite the most important centre in the south of England, and if he did so, he would certainly not have left such a large town without doing his best to spread the Gospel there.

But events were happening in Europe which culminated in the overthrow of the Roman Empire. The plains in Central Asia were drying up, and hordes of barbarians from there were being driven gradually westward, and they were driving out the inhabitants of European countries, until at last even the gates of Rome itself were being attacked, and so the legions had to be withdrawn from Gaul and Britain. Now, the Romans had never mixed with the British to any very great extent; true, a few of them had married British wives, but the admixture was never very great considering the length of time they were in Britain. They apparently held themselves as a superior race, and considered the Britons far below them in status, fit only for slaves or servants, so that when they withdrew they left no ties behind them such as might have been expected after nearly four hundred years of occupation.

No sooner had the Romans gone - perhaps even before they finally left - than the people of central and eastern Britain were subjected to attack from the Silures and other tribes from the west, who had never been really subjected by the Romans. These attacks were followed by raids from the Picts in the north, who now found Hadrian's wall either not defended at all or only very perfunctorily so.

Then came the Teutonic races, Jutes, Angles, and Saxons, driven from Europe by the barbarians from the east, who gradually overwhelmed the British. But there was a difference; the Teutons came to settle rather than to conquer, and although on occasion very warlike and thorough soldiers, they were primarily agriculturists, and from the first they intermixed with the Britons and settled on the land.

The Saxons made their way into the country, chiefly by way of the rivers, and appear to have made no use at all of the wonderful network of roads left by the Romans, and it seems a most remarkable thing that in spite of the fact that the Britons even before the Roman occupation had been accustomed to use carts and chariots, wheeled conveyances seem to have almost completely disappeared, and were not used on the roads again for at least a thousand years. So these splendid Roman roads became overgrown with grass and heather, and were eventually completely lost.

Near Crowthorne there was a cutting and a corresponding embankment, which stood until a few years ago, but vandal hands with no respect for the past have found it a very useful quarry for material for constructing modern houses, and now 1 am afraid that nearly, if not all, of the embankment has disappeared.

At Bannisters, near Finchampstead, is preserved a Roman milestone, which stood near by for nearly two thousand years.

With regard to the cut stone used for facing the walls and houses of Calleva Atrebatum, much of it was undoubtedly carted away and used locally, and must have proved a fine quarry in a district naturally devoid of stone suitable for building, but a great deal of it was used in the building of Reading Abbey, and this stone after the dissolution of the Abbey was conveyed down the river to

Windsor, where it was used in the building of the "Poor Knights' Houses." There it stands to-day, a lasting memorial of the thoroughness with which the Romans carried out their undertakings.

FOX HILL CLUMP

Photo: R.W. End

CHAPTER IV

CHOBHAM COMMON: AN ANCIENT MONUMENT

CHOBHAM Common! What magic there was in those two words to us when we were children! How different was that wild spot in those days from what it is now! How we enjoyed wandering over that great expanse of heather and strange wild flowers. How we used to look in the boggy spaces for the feathery wild cotton grass and the sundew fly traps, which were especially numerous in a part that we called "Russia" - not from any fancied resemblance to that great country, but because it was there that we gathered the rushes from which we made innumerable mats and other small articles. How the peewits hovered over our heads, feigning an excitement which fully convinced us that we must be near their nests, and with their clamouring drawing us far away in the wrong direction! How we used to search for the nests of the skylarks singing over our heads! Sometimes we were fortunate enough to find one, but were never allowed to disturb it. Once we found the nest of a golden-crested wren hanging from a willow branch, a bird not common in these parts. Often in a gorse bush we would find the nest of a linnet, well protected by the spikes of the bush, and now and then we would come across a grass snake sunning itself on the banks, and sometimes we would find the cast-off skins of some of these reptiles, than which no better whip could be found for our whip tops. How we raced and tore about in the heather, heedless of scratches and torn clothing, and without a thought of the past when the monks of Chertsey had crossed these self-same wilds taking their bees out to gather in the delicious heather honey, of which, judging from the extent of the remains of their apiary, they must have been very fond.

For hours we would wander, playing at all sorts of games, and heedless of the miles we traversed, feeling no weariness until the time came for us to turn our steps homewards, when suddenly there would come upon us such a tired feeling that we could hardly drag one foot after the other, and we would finally reach home half dead with fatigue, but by the next day all the weariness would be forgotten, and if only it had not been a school day, we would have been quite ready to repeat the performance.

And then those glorious days when there were troops encamped on the common, and we had the luck to be on the ground when a field day was in progress, or the day after, when we could pick up innumerable empty cartridge cases, which we would take home, smelling strongly of gunpowder, and play with for hours on wet days when it was impossible to go out, drilling them as soldiers, making them fight mimic battles, garrisoning miniature fortresses with them, and getting as much or even more amusement out of them than the most finished and expensive set of toy soldiers could have afforded.

And in the winter, when the water which had collected in the clay pits was frozen hard, what glorious slides could be made, and when the frost was still harder, there was skating on the duck ponds, which were safe long before Virginia Water bore, and they had the added advantage of being shallow, so that if the ice did give way, there was little danger of anything worse than wet trouser legs; and at night if the moon was shining how glorious it was, and even if there was no moon, there were generally enough dead branches of pinewood lying about to provide material for abundance of torches, and what can be more exciting than skating or dancing on the ice by torch-light? Now, alas! the duck ponds, which were made by the troops encamped on the common when they were mobilising for the Crimean War, if they still exist, are on enclosed ground, and the youth of to-day know little of the glories of the common of fifty or more years ago.

I am afraid that the recollections of my youth have led me somewhat astray from the subject of this chapter, which was intended to be on a monument which has long since disappeared, but which I believe to have been one of the very earliest symbols of Christianity ever erected in these islands. I am not sure of the exact spot where it stood, for all trace of it has long been lost, but I think it must have been near to, or perhaps on the very spot where there is a clump of pines, known as "Foxhill Clump" on the right hand side of the road leading to Chobham, plainly visible from the railway; and my reasons for thinking this are, that a prominent position for such a monument would naturally have been selected and that it was on this hill that the boundary of the Chertsey Abbey lands was shown.

St. Augustine first preached at Canterbury in A.D. 587, and sixty-nine years after that the Abbey of Chertsey was founded, and the Cross I speak of was sufficiently well known at that time to have become a landmark by which the boundary of the Abbey lands could be marked. In the grant to Frithwald dated 666 it is spoken of as the "Menechene Rude" (Monk's Cross), and was apparently old, even then.

There are two ways in which it might have been placed there.

A monk, or community of monks, may have made their way from Canterbury and built the cross there. The obstacles to such a journey would have been almost insurmountable, and the way would have been dangerous from many causes, and there would seem to have been little object in placing a monument in such a deserted spot, for beyond the cow-keepers at Coworth, and perhaps a few wandering swineherds or shepherds, the surrounding country for some distance was entirely uninhabited during the

Saxon occupation, until the erection of Chertsey Abbey. So personally I think it may have been there long before St. Augustine's time.

That there were already Christians in Britain cannot be doubted. Bertha, Queen of Ethelbert, was a Christian, which probably accounts for the friendly welcome which St. Augustine received on his arrival in this country.

During the Roman occupation, some, probably a good many, Christians must have settled in Britain. Among them were Claudia, a British lady married to Pudens, a Roman governor of the port of Chichester, probably the friends of St. Paul, mentioned in his second Epistle to Timothy (II Timothy 4, 12). It is hardly likely that there would be a second Pudens and Claudia, so that I think we are quite safe in assuming that they were the same. It is believed by many that St. Paul visited them at Chichester (Regnum), when he would undoubtedly have preached the Gospel there, where they would most certainly have gathered a Christian community round them.

Be this as it may, it gives us a possible explanation of the Monk's Cross, which I for one think a more likely one than an almost impossible journey with such a load through the forests and across the wastes from Canterbury.

Chichester was an important port of the Romans, and from it led a military road, which joined the road from London to Silchester at, or near, Duke's Hill at Bagshot. The road from Silchester to London passed right through Sunningdale, and, in fact, there seems to have been for a time a strong camp here, probably during the construction of the road. What, then, is more likely than that the monk or monks (presuming that they were monks) who erected the cross should have come from Chichester up this great road, and have placed it in a prominent position overlooking the encampment? I think this a very likely solution of the mystery of its erection, the more so as after the Saxon occupation the roads became derelict and wheeled traffic disappeared for centuries, and therefore it would have been extremely difficult, if not absolutely impossible, to convey heavy stones to such a position. Had it been of Saxon origin one would naturally have expected to find it near to the banks of a river, as it was the Saxon custom to convey heavy articles by water wherever possible.

The centuries in their passing have brought many changes. The Cross has long ago disappeared, no one knows exactly where it stood, but there it was, a landmark probably for centuries, reminding passers by on the heath, both of the Great Sacrifice and of the bounds of the Abbey lands, plainly to be seen for miles, for in those days the country round here was open, and so much less wooded than it is to-day that where there were trees or shrubs the localities were named after them. But although the cross itself is gone, and I have found few people who had ever even heard of it, its existence has given the name to two roads, Mincing Lane and Mincing Ride, both of which are derived from the "Menechene Rude" of Saxon days.

Photo: R.W. End

COWORTH PARK

Photo: R.W. End

THE FARM, COWORTH PARK

CHAPTER V

COWORTH

A SAXON Homestead! What was it like?

It is perhaps rather difficult for us in these days to realise the conditions under which our Saxon forefathers existed, but let us try to picture to ourselves what the household at Coworth may have been like.

So far as we can tell to-day, it consisted of one large room or hall, with immensely thick mud walls, strengthened and held together with interlaced sticks, and a thatched roof, which may or may not have been lined with rough boards, and with an opening at one end to let out the smoke from a wood fire, which, however, had a nasty habit of making a circuit of the whole building before finding its way into the open air.

Hollowed out of the wall at one end was a recess which could be more or less shut off from the hall by curtains. This was the ladies' bower, where they could retire when they wanted a little privacy and where they slept. In one of the side walls was a similar recess, which was occupied by the lord and lady of the house.

The furniture was of the simplest, consisting of a large, rough-hewn "board" or table top, which, when not in use, could be stood on edge against the wall, and when required was placed on trestles to form a table. In the centre was hollowed out a recess for the salt. Above this, on a slightly raised platform, sat the lord and his family and guests, and below this the servants both indoor and outdoor. The only other furniture consisted of stools, and perhaps a rough chair or two for the lord and ladies of the family.

The floor, of beaten clay, was covered with rushes, and generally several dogs wandered about, picking up odd scraps of food thrown to them at meal times. When the rushes were sodden with dirt and refuse, more were thrown down on top of them, so that when the hall had been in use for a few years, what with the smoke and the state of the floor, the conditions are better imagined than described. No wonder that in spite of a very high birth-rate the population did not appreciably increase!

The Saxons drank large quantities of beer, and after the lord and ladies had retired, drinking would still go on amongst the servants, who slept where they fell! Such was the ordinary Saxon household, and I have no doubt that this was the kind that first existed at Coworth.

The Saxons, being primarily an agricultural people, did not spend much time indoors. Their pursuits took them out into the open most of the time, which was perhaps just as well, considering the conditions under which they lived.

Meat was roasted on spits, and was brought to the table still on the spit. Large slices of bread were placed on the board, and each of the diners, commencing with the lord, taking the joint into his hand, hacked off such portions as he required with his dagger or seax, and laid them on the bread, which sucked up the gravy. From time to time portions were thrown to the dogs, who, when the meal was over, were regaled with the remnants of the sodden bread. Vegetables were practically unknown, so scurvy was rife. In the winter food was very scarce indeed, for, there being no roots to feed the cattle on, they were very thin and skinny, and hardly fit for food during the cold months when there was little or no grass for them.

But I am inclined to think that before the Saxons came to Coworth it was occupied, because we first trace it under the name "Herdies" in the grant to Chertsey Abbey. Probably a family or tribe of Angles settled at Englefield Green, and cultivated it, thus it became the "Anglefield," and casting their eyes on the beautiful grassy slope from Shrubs Hill, then called "Thornihull," saw that it would be good for grazing, and turned out their cattle there. They, in turn, were displaced by Saxons, who made it their Cow Garth, hence the present name.

There is little documentary evidence of the early days of Coworth, but we get a note of it in the Inquisition Post Mortem of Galfrid de Bagsete in the reign of Henry III, where it is stated that "he held of the King in capite certain lands towards 'Cowurthe' in serjeanty, in connection with lands at Sunninghull," for which he paid to the King 60s. annually.

Probably by this time Coworth was developing into a hamlet of small dwellings about Blacknest, for in the 29th year of Edward III (1356), a fine was collected in relation to a house at Coworth on its transfer from Johes Fraure and his wife to Johnes le Neve.

It could not have been very long after this that Coworth, which then covered a very much larger area than now, came into the possession of the Darenfords, afterwards called "Danford," for in the forty-fifth year of Edward III (1372) "William Darenford of Coworthe and Johanna his wife, conveyed to Wm. Podenhale, citizen of London, one messuage and forty acres of land and four acres of marsh in Coworth and Sunninghill." And in the same year Wm. Podenhale also had a conveyance from "Laur," the son of William Darenforde, of certain lands. These conveyances were, in all probability, in relation to the land now known as Titness Park, but it is impossible to say definitely just where they were situated.

The Derenfords were at Coworth for many generations, for in 1667 John, the son of Richard Darenford, was baptized at

Sunninghill, and in 1688 a John Danford of Coworth was buried there, indicating an uninterrupted occupation of over 300 years. In Norden's Survey in the reign of James I, is mentioned "Dornford" a ford across the brook, somewhere about the place where the bridge at Blacknest now stands; this was evidently named from the family owning it.

But during a portion at least of this time, Coworth appears to have been shared by the Lanes. The first authentic information we get of occupation by the Lanes is in 1571, when a son of Henry Lane of Coworth was baptized in Sunninghill Church. This Henry Lane probably attained affluence by marrying into one of the great Forest families, for doubtless it was he who "attended Henry VIII as a voluntier at the taking of Bulloigne" and married "Anne Norris, descended of ye noble family of Norris, and near kinsman unto Sir John Norris, Generall of ye forces in Ireland." On Lane's return from this glorious expedition he probably settled at Coworth, and some years later he purchased from Lord Norris the Manor of Sunninghill, which he did not keep long, for in 1583 he disposed of it to William Day of Eton.

The Lanes seem to have been a tough race, for in 1573 Henry Lane, probably the eldest son of the Henry Lane mentioned above, was married at Sunninghill to Amis Stoke. He died at Coworth in 1641, sixty-eight years after his marriage! His second brother, George, served under his great kinsman, Sir John Norris, in Ireland, where he married the daughter and sole heiress of Cormack O'Farrell of Killicroobagh. Their son, Richard Lane of Fulske, was made a baronet and married the only daughter of Gerald Fitzgerald of Clonbolg and Rathaman, one of the most noted of the old native patriots, and so became connected with the "fair Geraldine" of Surrey's dream.

Richard, son of Sir George Lane of Fulske, was Charles II's Principal Secretary of State for Ireland and was created Viscount Lanesborough.

The Lanes were at Coworth for over two hundred years, for in January, 1783, some members of a gang of ruffians who had been carrying out a series of depredations on the surrounding heaths, were tracked to the Wells Inn at Sunninghill, where young Edward Lane, son of Edward Lane of

Coworth, was shot to death in endeavouring to arrest them, as shown by the Register of Sunninghill Church, where he was buried.

The Lanes seem to have occupied what is now the Farm House at Coworth, which they probably built for themselves when they first came there. This house, although it has undoubtedly been altered from time to time, is an excellent example of a Tudor farmhouse. It faces the west, and is built of oak, brick and plaster work, with picturesque gable wings. From the high roof rises a good chimney stack. The rooms are low-pitched, with the usual heavy beams across the ceilings, and are approached by narrow passages at different elevations. The massive rough-hewn oak beams show how plentiful that material must have been in this neighbourhood in those days.

Here lived, and was probably born, in 1616, the Edward Lane, who, living until 1714, accomplished what could not have been possible in any other period since the Conquest, for he witnessed the reigns of ten sovereigns, or rather sovereign rulers, James I, Charles I, the Commonwealth, the Protectorates of Oliver Cromwell and his son

Richard, Charles II, James II, William and Mary, Anne, and George I.

In the list of the Feet of Fines for Berkshire there is an entry in the Easter Term of 31 George II (1758) as follows: "Robert Tunstall and Samuel Baldwin and Robert Harlans, Esq., and Susannah, wife: House, etc., and lands in the hamlet of Coworth in the parish of Old Windsor."

I have no definite information as to what portion of Coworth this relates, but I think it was in connection with the transfer of the land on which the Nursery is built, and probably extended from Kiln Lane, the boundary of the Tittenhurst property, down to the corner at Holly Cottage. All this land was, I believe, for many years in the eighteenth century, nursery gardens.

In 1796 Coworth was purchased by James Barwell, Esq. (son of William Barwell, Esq., formerly Governor of Bengal and a staunch friend of Warren Hastings) who built the present mansion by adding wings to an older house. It has, however, been much added to since his time. He, or his brother, also built Buckhurst.

While the new house was building, Mr. Barwell probably resided at the old Tudor Farm, for some years ago, when some old oak panelling was being removed, a curious old Indian native coin was found behind it.

Mr. Barwell died in 1811, when Coworth passed to James Smith Baber, Esq., of Sunninghill Park, who let it to Mr. Nettleship.

In 1840, just about the time our church was being built, Coworth again changed hands, the purchaser being John Alves Arbuthnot, Esq., and I am informed by Mr. Kettle that while it was in Mr. Arbuthnot's occupation a large quantity of charcoal was found buried near the Roman Road. How it came to be deposited there is a mystery, but the Romans used charcoal both for heating their houses and for industrial purposes. No traces of a Roman villa have ever been found near by where this charcoal was found, but recently Mr. Young showed me a pair of horse-shoes which were found on the hill above. One of them was dug from under an oak tree, the stem of which was about two feet thick, which indicates that they must have been there for a very long time, I submitted these shoes to the curator of the Reading Museum to see if he could say whether they were Roman, but he thought there was rather too much iron left in them, although the pattern was exactly similar to some Roman ones we compared them with. When told just where they had been found, I thought it quite possible that they may have been of Roman origin, and that the dry sand protected by the trees had wonderfully preserved them. The finding of these shoes made me wonder if, at the time the road was in use, there might have been a farrier's shop by the roadside, which would account for the dump of charcoal?

Although very nearly the whole of Coworth was in Old Windsor Parish, and only one small corner of it in Sunninghill, Old Windsor was so far away that the owners more or less considered themselves parishioners of Sunninghill, and were benefactors to the church there, but now that we had a church at Sunningdale, conditions were altered, and from the time he came to Coworth until his death in 1873, Mr. Arbuthnot took great interest in our church and schools. In addition to being a liberal subscriber to both these institutions, he gave the first organ to the church, which was used until the installation of the present instrument, when it was sold to the Congregational Church, where it did duty for some years, and then was sold to a church in the north of England. I think he also gave the bell, which has recently been replaced by a larger one given by Mrs. Sanday.

Mr. Arbuthnot was succeeded by his son, Mr. William Arbuthnot, who, in 1884, disposed of the estate to Mr. (afterwards Sir William) Farmer, who was also very much interested in our church, and it was largely through his influence that while he was churchwarden, the nave was rebuilt, a costly and substantial work, for which he found more than half the funds. He also replaced the organ by the present one.

Sir William Farmer would very much have liked to close the little-used road through Coworth from Shrubs Hill to Blacknest, and had he done so without saying anything to anybody, I think no one would have interfered with his so doing, but not considering this a fair thing, he called a meeting of parishioners and made very handsome offers of compensation for the road. His thus opening up the question was unfortunate, for people who had no interest whatever in the road, which they seldom or never used, opposed its closing, and so lost to Sunningdale for ever the benefits which were so freely offered. One of the objectors did not know where the road was, and had never been through it.

Lord Stanley, now the Right Hon. the Earl of Derby, K.G., K.C.V.O., etc., purchased Coworth about forty years ago. He also has been a benefactor to the church and schools and other institutions. Unfortunately owing to his numerous public engagements, he is able to spend very little time with us in Sunningdale, but has shown a very lively interest in the affairs of the parish; one of his acts being the unveiling of the War Memorial some years ago.

CHAPTER VI

BROOMHALL NUNNERY

HOW many of us, I wonder, have ever tried to picture Sunningdale as it was at the time of the Norman Conquest? I imagine it to have been a vast, undulating, heathy waste in the forest, almost treeless except at Shrubs Hill, and perhaps with one or two large oaks in the neighbourhood of Windlesham and at Coworth, where they were more or less protected from deer and swine. Here and there were patches of grass where the heather had been burned off, or where the grass was stronger than the heath. No houses with the exception of the great hall at Coworth, and perhaps here and there a rude hut constructed of turf, inhabited by swineherds and gooseherds from the great Abbeys of Chertsey and Windsor.

Much of the ground must have been marsh, and to the west was a vast lake, the shallows of which probably dried up in summer. From this lake ran two streams, one of which has completely disappeared with the gradual drying up of the greater portion of the lake, although it must have been of some importance, as evidenced by the finding of the remains of a landing stage some fifty years ago in the gardens of St. Bruno, and the traces showing the width of its former bed.

This stream apparently led down through what is now the Rise, through Sunningdale Park, and most likely all that now remains of it is the small stream running through the grounds of Dale Lodge by the side of Kiln Lane, where traces of its former bed are clearly visible.

The other is our brook, which was also very much larger centuries ago, as shown by the nature of its surroundings.

The district teemed with red and fallow deer, wild boars, and various kinds of wild fowl, and no doubt it was owing to this that the neighbourhood was so open and treeless, for the deer browsed on the young plants and the boars rooted them up.

The views from the higher ground must have been extensive, had there been people to enjoy them, for even now, surrounded as we are by woods and houses, one can see for many miles from the hill above the Golf Links, generally known as the "Black Hill." Both from there and from the brow of the hill at Portnall Park one could see the Crystal Palace and Epsom Downs on a clear day. Looking to the south east from these hills in those days, one would most likely be able to see not far off the stately pile of Chertsey Abbey, which had been founded some four hundred years before the Conquest, and whose extensive lands ran very nearly to the place where Sunningdale station now stands. The monks of Chertsey must have been very fond of the delicious heather honey - probably it was the only means they had of sweetening food - for traces of a large apiary can, I believe, still be seen on Chobham Common.

The sunny slopes by Sunningdale station were then known as "Hertleys," most probably from their being the favourite haunt of the wild deer, and under this name are mentioned in the grant of land to the Abbey.

All the books on English history that I have read seem to convey the impression that our Norman rulers were hard, ruthless men, cruel, stern warriors, caring for nothing but their own advancement and their hunting, but there is plenty of evidence to show that, stern and hard though they were, there were other sides to their character. William the Conqueror had no doubt inherited from his grandfather, the Tanner, strong business instincts. His conquest of England was undertaken as a business proposition. He considered, and probably rightly, that he had a better title to the throne of England than the son of Earl Godwin, and had undoubtedly been recognised by Edward as his rightful successor. Be this as it may, it was his business genius that made England into one united kingdom, and that when this was accomplished provided us with a record in the Domesday Book such as no other country can boast of - a record which has been of inestimable value for nearly nine hundred years.

Then again, our Norman monarchs must have been intensely religious men, carrying the same vigour into their religion as into their warlike pursuits. This is shown by the number of churches, monasteries, and other religious houses that were built. When we remember that the whole population of the country was only about two millions, and look round on all the fine buildings we have left, and allow something for natural decay and wilful destruction that must have taken place, and the length of time that even simple operations must have taken to do in the absence of machinery, I think it is a very conservative estimate to say that at least one-half of the men must have been engaged directly and indirectly in building churches and other places devoted to religious exercises. With an eye to future development many of these churches were of enormous size, out of all proportion to the population of the districts they were intended to serve, but some were quite small.

The reign of Henry I showed special activity in this direction, and it was probably then that the little Norman church at Sunninghill, dedicated to St. Michael and All Angels, was erected.

It is impossible to say when exactly the nunnery at Broomhall was founded, for many of the records seem to have been destroyed in a disastrous fire in 1462. But from what evidence there is, it would appear to have been founded some time in the twelfth century. Some say that it was founded by a member of the royal family, but the only reliable evidence of this appears to be that in a petition of the sixteenth century it is described as having been "founded by the King's progenitors," a phrase that may have been used with the object of influencing His Majesty. That it was in existence in the twelfth century is shown by the gift to it by King John in the first year of his reign (1199) of the church at Sunninghill.

As the church seems to have been in existence for some time, it is probable that the nunnery did not come into being until towards the end of the century, as it seems likely that, had it been of earlier foundation, the gift would have been made before - I assume this from the fact that most such houses were either built in connection with an existing church, or had one added to them very soon after their foundation. But, however that may be, the fact remains that it was certainly in existence in 1199, and it seems for many centuries to have been under the patronage of the monarchs and their queens, probably owing to the fact that Sunninghill Church was in the Manor of Cookham, which was always considered the possession of the queen for the time being.

As to the nunnery having been founded by a member of the royal family, there is, as I have said, but little evidence of this, and I think that it is quite as likely to have been founded by the De Warrene family, for although it was built in Windsor Forest, it was on land occupied by Earl de Warrene.

The De Warrenes were closely allied to the royal family, were great benefactors to the Benedictine Order, and were founders of the Priory of Lewes, the chief Cluniac house in England. The first Earl, William, had married Gunreda, the half-sister of Henry I; and Matilda's nephew, son of David I of Scotland, in 1139 married Ada, daughter of Earl Warrene.

But whether the nunnery was founded by royalty or not, there is plenty of evidence to show that it was under royal patronage from the first. At the beginning of its career it probably possessed little more than its actual site and was most likely dependent on the Abbey of Chertsey for its support, but the nuns soon increased their possessions, mainly by the piety of benefactors, but also by clearances and encroachments on the forest. King John not only gave them the church at Sunninghill, but also granted them a virgate of land in (Old) Windsor, probably the land now known as Broomhall Farm and the strip on which the school stands, including the land now used as allotments. On this a rent of forty pence was reserved, which was released in the reign of Henry III. The Farm of Windsor was charged in favour of the Sisterhood with a payment of 8s. 2½ d., and the halfpenny a day which they also had was raised to twopence. By 1227 their possessions had increased to:

- Fifty acres of marsh of the Manor of Windsor in Laverset above the water of Bagshot.
- Hartley, thirty acres of marshland in Hurley under Chabeham (Chobham),
- Twenty acres of marsh of the manor of Tottenhurst in the parish of Sunninghill, assarted. In the 23rd Henry III the quantity was increased to thirty acres, and the name is then written as "Tetenhurst."

In 1231 Henry III granted to the Prioress of Broomhall in perpetuity pannage for hogs in the King's forest at Windsor, and also three oak beams and an oak tree to make shingles for the repair of their refectory; but apparently not content with this, we find that encroachments were made by the Prioress on the royal demesne and "two hundred oaks and more were torn up, to the great damage of the crown." We also learn that the Prioress held by gift of the King's father 150 acres of the Forest at Winkfield, doubtless the manor of Chawbridge, which apparently they had already cultivated.

In the 26th Henry III directions were given to "Pay out of our treasury to Brother John, our almoner, to feed the poor for the soul of the Empress formerly our sister (Eleanor, the wife of the Emperor Frederick II of Germany) £8 6s. 8d., to feed two thousand poor persons, to wit, one half at Ankerwick and the other half at Bromhal."

An important acquisition in 1285 was the benefaction of Henry de Lacy, Earl of Lincoln, and his wife Margaret, of 100 acres of the waste of Asseridge, between Billingbere and the royal way which leads from Brackenhale (Old Bracknell) to Reading.

The earliest Egham Charter which relates to Broomhall is undated, but there seem to be indications that it was granted about 1249 or 1250. It records a gift by Gilbert, son of Richard de la Barr of Chertsey, to Juliana, prioress of Broomhall, of rents arising from land in Egham and a tenement there. Now the name of this Juliana does not appear in any of the existing lists of prioresses, but as the gift was confirmed later on to Agnes, who at present heads the list, and who was prioress in 1266, Juliana evidently preceded her. The witnesses were all local men who lived in the middle and towards the end of the thirteenth century, and several of them witnessed both the original charter and the confirmation, which is also undated, but contains a reference to proceedings at Guildford in 1271.

Two other undated grants to Agnes bear the names of some of the same witnesses: the first grants to Agnes from Richard de Thorpe lands and tenements in the parish of Egham, near the bridge of Staines in the Huche (the modern Hythe): the second is a gift by Robert de Scothe of a tenement at "le Knolle."

In 1308 the Church of Aldworth and its Vicarage was given to the Nunnery, together with certain crofts and virgates of land and tithes of mills and various small tithes, including those on apples, gardens, flax and cheese for the maintenance of the Vicar.

In 1391, in consideration of their poverty, they were allowed to appropriate the advowson of North Stoke in the county of Oxford, but the Priory had to pay on Christmas Day a pension of 3s. 4d. to the Dean and Chapter of Lincoln in recognition of their consent to the appropriation.

It is rather interesting to note that in 1246 Henry III granted a charter to the Prioress of Broomhall to build a new bridge over the stream. As this bridge is there spoken of as the "new brugge," it would seem to imply that there was a bridge even earlier than that. The question is, where was this bridge? Presumably its purpose was to enable the nuns to cross to their property on the other side of the stream, and particularly to their church at Sunninghill. In making a search for old bridleways, or in fact for anything else, we have to ignore all thought of boundaries and roads as they exist now. Boundaries particularly were most elastic, and often consisted of mere ridges of turf, easily removed. Bridle tracks were more important and permanent. They were frequently marked by rows of trees, planted on the sunny side to afford shade to wayfarers, and were often carried round the boundaries of fields or properties, and so it has come about that very often modern roads and footpaths follow the courses of old bridleways, although this is not by any means always the case. Now, from various indications, I have come to the conclusion that the old bridleway from the Nunnery to Sunninghill, entering by the corner near the Dutch Barns at Broomhall Farm, ran by way of the hedge across the Church Fields to the footpath through the fields, where it turned to the left, right on by the side of the row of trees to the private road in Coworth Park, and crossing the brook below the mill pond by the new bridge (most likely a wooden structure, which I fancy was built just about where the present bridge in Coworth stands), and so along Coworth Road, Sandy Lane and across Sunningdale Park and the Larch Avenue to the foot of the hill by Pembroke Lodge, and thence across to the church. The row of trees probably marked the Coworth boundary in those days, and on the lower side towards the brook was, I feel sure, the mill pond, and below it the mill, the site of which, by the kindness of Lord Derby (who has given us every facility for investigation), I think Mr. Reed and I have recently found.

I suppose that it is almost impossible for us in these days to realise fully the important place occupied by the religious houses in the Middle Ages. Manors were as nearly as possible self-supporting, and there was little communication between the different parts of the country. Roads, if any, were very few and bad; nearly all travelling was done on horseback or on foot. Quarrels and fighting between the Barons were frequent, and bands of outlaws were not uncommon. Inns, which became so important when roads had been improved and stage coaches came into existence, were unknown, or were very scarce. Wayfarers relied almost entirely on the religious houses for their necessary supplies, and for their night's lodging. All classes were accommodated, and those who could afford it gave gifts according to their means or generosity in return for their hospitality. The houses were open to rich and poor alike, although, naturally, the people of means chose the larger and better equipped ones when they could do so, for the sake of the better fare and better stabling for their horses.

Now, our little Nunnery at Broomhall was never a rich foundation, and was only a small one; probably the household never consisted of more than the Prioress and five or six nuns, and though in course of time the lands belonging to it became very extensive, yet most of it was so poor that it was of very little value from an agricultural point of view, and so was rather an incumbrance than otherwise.

There was a bridle-track running from London to Salisbury and Southampton, following, I believe, pretty much the line of our present main road, but this route was used chiefly by the poorer wayfarers, and as the Broomhall Nunnery was the only house of call between Ankerwyke and Basingstoke until the foundation of Hartley Wintney, it will readily be seen that the calls upon it were pretty heavy from the poorer classes of travellers, who could afford to give little or nothing in return for their accommodation. The wealthier travellers preferred to go a little out of their way to the more stately and important Abbey at Chertsey, which, like so many other places, became enormously rich on their gifts.

Unfortunately, many of these larger houses, as they grew in wealth, increased in avarice and, in many cases, seemed to lose sight of the reasons for their existence; from severity they turned to luxury and, so long as the monks fared well and waxed fat and lazy, they cared little how perfunctorily their duties were performed, and they had little sympathy for the difficulties of the smaller and poorer houses. Broomhall gives a striking instance of this lack of consideration, which is worth noticing.

There was a provision that the Abbey of Chertsey should supply the Nunnery with seven loaves, called miches, and seven gallons of convent ale weekly. No doubt this at first was freely given; but, as Chertsey became rich and even more rich, they more and more begrudged the help given to their poor neighbour until at last they thought fit to dispute it. The matter was referred to the arbitration of Cardinal Morton, Archbishop of Canterbury, and on February 16th, 1489, he gave his decision in favour of the nuns.

The monks of Chertsey seem to have been guilty of a very shabby trick - either before or after this arbitration, but exactly when is not quite clear. If before, it may have had some influence on the Archbishop's decision, if brought to his notice, as it naturally would have been. In any case, it became known some twenty years later, and during the interim the monks paid the corrody in one form or another, and then made another attempt to get out of it.

Jane (or Joan) Rawlyns, the last Prioress, had to fight the matter out again, and she appealed to Anne Thomas, one of her predecessors who had resigned in 1498, to help substantiate her claim. She wrote as follows:-

"The saying of Dame Anne Thomas some tyme prioresse of Broomhalle and now prioresse of Wintoney. Whiche saith that on Issabell Bealle whiche was prioresse there affore her and her predesessores tyme oute of mynde was seased of a corrodye or Als yerely ons in the weke was payed of vij case of covent brede and vij galantes of covent ale owte of the house or Abbaye of Charsey, fforthermore the said Dame Anne Thomas saith that ij monks of Charsey whoys names were Brampton and Berry came to the howse of Broomhalle and there desired the foresaid Issabell Beale which was prioresse there to shew unto theyme the evidence whereby they claymed and had yt corrodye or Alms and she brought forthe a faire writing in parchment to theyme under the covent seale of their Pallace of Charsey and when they had seen it and redde it over they cast it in the fire and brent it, whereof the said prioresse was right sory and muche displeased with theyme for the same, but not wt,standing she ynjoyed the said corrodie during her tyme.

"And then next after her came the said Anne Thomas and was prioresse ther and she had yerely during her tyme which was xiv yerys ever yere v quarters of whete payed by on Hatche which was servant wt. the said Abbot of Charsey Whiche Hatche at thys tyme is on lyve. And then next after her the said Dame Anne, as she saithe came on Dame Elizabeth Lakenore which was prioresse ther and that she had enjoyed the said whete during all her tyme."

Undoubtedly this tendency to greater luxury in the religious houses, and the wandering from their original purposes, was a very great factor in their doom. Much of the wealth of the country had come to them in one way or another, and thinking people had for many years been bound to come to the conclusion that this wealth, so easily obtained, was being greatly abused, and that the substance of religion was being sacrificed to empty forms, much as had been the case with the Jews at the time of the coming of Our Lord - so does history repeat itself. Congregations were practically excluded from some of the largest churches, because there was no room for them owing to the endless processions of monks and friars. Luxurious and immoral lives were being led by those whose duty it was to set a good example to the laity, and their duties either neglected or most perfunctorily performed. The arrogance and haughtiness of some of the larger houses was a byword, and they made so many enemies that many of them had to live in strongly fortified houses.

Colonel Cooper King tells an anecdote which shows clearly the luxury in which so many of the inmates of the larger houses lived. I have not his book before me, so must quote from memory.

"Henry VIII, when out hunting one day, lost his way in the forest, and finding that he was in the neighbourhood of Reading, decided to go to the Abbey, where he knew they kept a good table, for his dinner. He dined with the assembled monks, and ate heartily of his favourite dish - a sirloin of beef. After the repast, the Abbot, whose digestion seems to have been seriously impaired, remarked that he would give a hundred pounds to be able to enjoy such a hearty meal as the monarch had taken. Henry laughingly asked the Abbot if he was in earnest, and the Abbot replied that he certainly was, as owing to his poor digestion, he was quite unable to enjoy the pleasures of the table as he had once done.

"Shortly after, the Abbot was arrested and taken to the Tower of London, where, although no charge was preferred against him, he was strictly confined for several days and fed on a very meagre diet of bread and water. When this had gone on for some time, he was agreeably surprised one day by his attendants bringing in a large and perfectly cooked sirloin, which he attacked ravenously. As he finished a hearty meal, the curtains behind him parted and in came the King, who demanded £100 from him.

"When the Abbot remonstrated, saying that no charge had been brought against him. The King said:

" ' Did you not promise £100 to him who should restore your powers of digestion, so that you could enjoy such a meal as you have just partaken of?' "

"The Abbot made the best of the matter, and kept the terms of his rash promise."

But however much the larger houses may have wandered from their original course, the smaller ones, probably from want of means, do not seem to have followed their example, and there appears to have been no ground for complaint against our little community at Broomhall - at any rate in its later days, although possibly one of the earlier prioresses, Isabella de Sonnings, may have been of a somewhat quarrelsome disposition, for we find that in 1295 she quarrelled with Joan, wife of John de W'lveley, who complained of her to the authorities, whereupon Geoffrey de Picheford took ten beasts belonging to the nunnery and detained them for a fortnight against sureties and pledges, and that Isabella complained to the Queen, whereupon they were restored, but Phillips, the Porter of Windsor Castle, claimed seven shillings for their keep. Again in 1404 there seems to have been some unpleasantness, and a Commission was appointed to inquire into the matter, but after that there appears to have been no cause whatever for complaint. Yet it was one of the very earliest to be suppressed - probably because it was so small and defenceless.

But before its suppression it had evidently fallen into a bad financial position, for we find that much of its land had been let on very long leases, and can only conclude that such a disastrous course had been followed to obtain money paid down in a lump sum in consideration of such concessions. This was by no means an uncommon practice with such houses when they were in difficulties, neither was it an uncommon thing for the lessees to claim the land so leased as their own freehold, and it was by no means unusual for them to sell such lands and pocket the proceeds. Such appears to have been the case with Potnall, now Portnall, and the land surrounding it. This belonged to the nunnery at Broomhall, who leased it to two Egham men for a long period. Edward IV purchased it from them, and apparently the nuns did not think it worth while to try and get it back until Henry VIII declared himself a Defender of the Faith, when they seem to have thought they had a better chance of success, for they presented a petition to that monarch, unsuccessfully it would seem, for we find that he granted it to William Fitzwilliam in 1528, and it afterwards descended to his heirs. Land in Egham had also been let on lease for a long term, and when in 1568 the College granted a new lease, the tenants, who were descendants of the original lessees, claimed the freehold, and successfully, for the College does not appear as the owner after that date.

The suppression took place in 1521, two years after the suppression of the nunnery at Higham in Kent, but the cases were not exactly similar. In the case of Higham the house appears to have borne a very indifferent character, and was almost deserted, but the only fault to be found with

Broomhall seems to have been its poverty.

The official story was that the house became escheat to the King by voidance, but this was not quite correct. True, the Prioress resigned, but only under pressure from Richard Archprieste, a notary public employed by the Bishop of Salisbury. Evidently the resignation was not very easily obtained, for he writes: "With great adoe the nuns are got from Broomhall," which seems to imply at least some reluctance on the part of the nuns to leave the place which they had so long enjoyed.

The last Prioress was Joan Rawlyns, and she was supposed to have been paid 20 nobles down, and was promised a pension of £5 a year, which she seems to have had some difficulty in getting, at any rate for the first year or two, but she was still drawing it in 1545. There seems also to have been difficulty and delay in getting the documents from the Bishop of Salisbury.

Fisher is said to have paid £300 for the "mortmayning" of Higham and Broomhall, so the crown was no loser by the transaction, but apparently Henry VIII was not content with this, for he cast his eye upon Knowle Grove with a view to throwing it into Windsor Forest. A valuation was made and its extent was found to be 44 acres one rood, and the timber on it worth £16 16s. The King appears to have driven a close bargain, for he paid for the whole, timber included, only £44 12s. During the reign of Mary or Elizabeth the College tried to get it back. Their petition, which is undated, diplomatically ignores the fact that Henry acquired it by purchase, but as the sale was entered in the records the petition was of course refused.

As I have said, many of the earlier records were apparently destroyed in a disastrous fire, and it is probably owing to this cause that we cannot give with any degree of certainty the names of the earliest prioresses. Quite possibly no records were kept for the first few years - but on the authority of Dugdale and others it would appear that the following is as complete a list as can now be traced:-

1266, Agnes was Abbess. Her name also occurs in 1268, but as she was given a grant of tithes in 1266, the earlier date must be the correct one. Perhaps her appointment was not confirmed until 1268.

1281, Margery de Wycumbe, elected November 9th. 1295, Isabelle de Sonninges, who resigned in 1310.

1310 to 1321, uncertain.

1321, Matilda de Burgton or Broughton. It is quite likely that Matilda or some other member of her family may have presided between 1310 and 1321, as the de Burgtons were very great benefactors to the nunnery.

1336, Gunilda, who is also mentioned in 1348, soon after which date she resigned.

1348, Isabella de Hougheford, who is also mentioned in 1350.

1358, Alicia de Falle.

1373, Alienora. She may have been the same person known as Eleanor Burton, who seems to have resigned in 1402.

1402 or 1403, Juliane Dunne.

1405, Thomasia or Thomadine Bodington. She is also mentioned in 1413, 1419, and 1430.

1437, Alice Burton, whose name occurs again in 1445.

1461, Isabella Beale.

1483, Anne Thomas, who was promoted to the Priory of Wintney, Hants, in 1489.

1492, Anna or Elizabeth Lewkenor.

1511, Joan Rawlyns, who surrendered in 1521.

So ended the career of Broomhall as a nunnery. So far as we can say after this long interval of time, it had served its purpose as a refuge for wayfarers for the long period it had been in existence (very nearly three centuries) nobly and well; it had succoured the poor in spite of its own poverty, and had kept its head up with hardly a breath of scandal. But a new era was dawning, and perhaps the time had come when it could no longer serve any useful purpose; but whether such was the case or not, the end had come, and now its revenues, such as they were, were to be diverted into a new channel of usefulness.

The estates of the nunnery were adjudged escheat to the crown, and were by letters patent dated 21st October, 1522, granted, together with the Rectory and advowson of the church at Sunninghill, to St. John's College, Cambridge. This grant was confirmed by a Bull from Clement VII. in 1524. On receiving this Bull, the College set about the appointment of a local agent for the administration of their newly acquired property, and Thomas Warde of Winkfield was selected to act for them. The manor of Chawbridge was let on lease to Richard Warde, clerk of the poultry to the King. Broomhall and Tittenhurst to Oliver Lowthe, who was succeeded by Henry Atlee and Anthony Batlie. These tenants seem to have been practical and working farmers, but the next one might perhaps be better described as a "gentleman farmer," for in 1564 it was let for forty years at a rent of £7 6s. 8d. to "Roger Ascham of London, gentleman, the Queen's Latin Secretary."

But Roger Ascham was an elderly man when he became the tenant of Broomhall, and probably his scholarly pursuits had not fitted him for the arduous life of a farmer, and much as we would have liked to think of the old gentleman walking over his fields and trying in his scholarly way to discover the secrets of nature, I am afraid that as a matter of fact he never lived here, although he probably visited his farm from time to time, for from 1558, when Queen Elizabeth came to the throne, he seems to have been in constant attendance on her, and to have resided at court until his death in December, 1568. He was buried at St. Sepulchre's Church.

He was perhaps the greatest scholar of his day, and wrote several notable books. One of them, "The Schoolmaster," was said by Dr. Johnson to be the best ever written as a guide to the study of languages. Unfortunately he seems to have been somewhat of a gambler, and a patron of the cruel sport of cockfighting. But his favourite sport seems to have been the more innocent one of archery, and in 1545 he published "Toxophilus," a treatise on that sport, which is perhaps the best ever written on the subject, and even yet well worth perusal by those interested in archery.

On the death of Roger Ascham, his widow appears to have parted with the lease of Broomhall to Thomas Bennett, a yeoman of Heckfield, Hants, who in turn transferred the lease, which had apparently been extended, to Christopher Heneage and his wife Anne. The lease expired in 1618, and another was granted to them for a period of 21 years.

Mrs. Fradgley has recently informed me that Broom Hall, as it is now called, was rebuilt in the early part of the seventeenth century (1610-1620) so that it must have been some time during the occupation of the Heneages that this work was undertaken. Probably some other work was done at about the same time, as I have seen buildings of about the same age in which similar materials were used, in Sunningdale, some of which have now been pulled down.

In 1634 the College decided to annex Broom Hall to the mastership. This was no great gift at the time, but if it has not been rescinded, it must now provide a large income for the Master, while the College itself apparently struggles on with difficulty in making both ends meet.

In a terrier of 1634, giving a list of things belonging to Sunninghill Church, is included "one annuity or set portion of money per annum, 40s., paid half-yearly out of a certain farme called Broomhall, which ye College of St. John's at Cambridge hath lying neare unto our church, and is of our parish in all taxes and rates whatsoever; though not in our parish." This curious state of affairs caused a good deal of friction between the parishes of Egham and Sunninghill. In 1730 came threats, and there is an entry in the Vestry Book at Sunninghill as follows:-

"Resolved that if the parish of Egham make any distraint on Broom hall Farm or commence any law suit thereupon, to defend the said law suit."

The affair came to a head two years later, when Egham Vestry distrained for rates and seized a cow. Both parishes seem to have been in a rather excited state, and both seemed to be certain of the justice of their cause. Litigation followed, and both sides had to borrow money for expenses.

Evidently legal proceedings were not much more speedy in those days than they are now, for it seems to have taken three years to get a settlement in favour of Sunninghill.

Egham borrowed their money from a Mr. Crockford, and some of the items of their expenditure are interesting:-

"1736. Journey to Abington (Abingdon) Assizes, the expenses paid by Mr. Mackason and John Rolfe out of the £21 borrowed of Mr. Crockford.

"July 4th Paid all ye bills at Abington which are now in John Rolfe's hands.

	£ s. d.
Spent at Henley going down to Abington	1 10 6
At Abington for eating and drinking, five meals	2 5 1
Paid for ye horses at Abington, five horses	1 12 6
Paid at Henley coming back	1 5 0
Paid before we came to Henley for Turnpikes and spent . . .	0 2 6

Spent at Benson	0 2 6
Paid Mr. Greenway for Council ...	5 5 0
Paid Stephen Perrin and Field	1 11 6
Paid R. Hart and Mr. West	1 11 6
Paid Turnpike	0 0 9
Paid for wine	0 2 0
Paid four horses hire	1 10 0
For Mr. Rolfe and Mr. Mackason ..	2 0 0
Paid Will May	0 6 6
Paid William Chips	0 4 6
Spent and paid when we were at Broomhall with Mr. Lyward and Samuel Very to View the bounds ..	0 5 0
Mr. Mackason spent at ye King's Head when Mr. Sawyer was there with the Vestry	0 6 0
Mr. Mackason spent at ye Hut (Broomhall Hut) when the witnesses went to View the bounds	0 3 0½
Richard Rolfe spent at Broadways upon Mr. Sawyer	0 6 6
Paid Edward Hart and Thomas Porter	0 9 0

	£20 19 4½
John Rolfe in hand	0 0 7½

Details of some of these items might make interesting reading. Anyhow, they seem to have had some " wet " days, but perhaps that was only natural at a time when Vestry meetings were held in public houses and it was found necessary to limit the expenditure of public money on "refreshments" to a shilling each for those present, and when it was customary to broach barrels of ale in the churchyard on Thanksgiving Day; perhaps, though, there was some excuse for this latter custom, as many of the congregation came from very long distances.

Sunninghill seems to have rejoiced very much over their victory, for we find the following entries:-

"April 7th 1735. Paid ringers for ringing the bells after the tryall 5s., and £8 towards the law expenses of John Baber, Esq., Mr. Aldridge £8." A year afterwards they again rang the bells for two days, for which they paid 6s., and two years after they paid further sums of £10 each to Mr. Baber and the son of Mr. Aldridge, which was apparently a final settlement of the debt incurred for the case.

Mr. Baber had a direct interest in the settlement of this law suit, as he was the tenant of Broomhall and Tittenhurst.

The next change to come to Broomhall was the making of the Staines and Wokingham Railway, cutting right through it, in the early fifties of last century, which divided up the land, and was the direct cause of the letting out of portions of it on building leases - the first place so let, I understand, being for the purpose of building the Station Hotel, and the second Oak Lodge (now Holmwood).

No doubt many have wondered at the large curve taken by the railway across Chobham Common. The original intention was, I believe, to have taken the railway in a straight line from Virginia Water to Ascot, which would have brought Sunningdale station somewhere near the church, but Colonel Challoner, who then owned Portnall Park, strongly opposed its passing through his land, and I have been told kept several men on duty to keep the surveyors out of his grounds, with the result that an alternative route had to be taken. No opposition to the new route seems to have been made by St. John's College. Perhaps they had sufficient vision to see how the construction of the railway must eventually considerably enhance the value of their estate.

And now the story of Broomhall, so far as I know it, is nearly told.

Many people have farmed it, but the land is poor and few I think have found it profitable; gradually wheat and oat fields have given way to grass, until now it is only used as a dairy farm, and I believe no attempt at all is made to grow grain.

In 1890 a skeleton was found when digging for the foundations of the Dutch Barns in the paddock. The *Windsor and Eton Express* gives the following account of this discovery in their issue of July 12th, 1890:-

"A few days ago, some men in the employ of Mr. Wm. Farmer, of Coworth Park, were engaged at Broomhall Farm in digging some foundations for a building to be erected in the rick yard of the farm. In the course of this work part of the remains of a human skeleton were found embedded in the soil about two feet below the surface, the portions discovered consisting of a leg, an arm, finger and other bones. Some of the old servants on the estate state that they have always been given to understand that the site was formerly a Roman burial ground. If so this would account for the discovery of human remains in the present instance. Antiquarians may perhaps throw some light on the subject."

The *Reading Standard* had, I believe, a fuller description, and the following week gave a report on the inquest which was held on these remains, but unfortunately I have not been able to get access to these papers. Needless to say, the remains were not Roman but mediaeval, and people came hastily to the conclusion that the paddock was a graveyard belonging to the old nunnery. This I think very unlikely for two reasons, the first being that as the nuns had already a burying ground attached to their church at Sunninghill it would not be necessary, and the second is that had it been kept as a graveyard during the time that Broomhall was used as a nunnery, it would have been reserved and treated as consecrated ground, for few burial grounds in use up to the sixteenth century have been desecrated with the exception of some in large towns where land was badly needed for building on, or for open spaces. Here, where land was of little value, there would be no temptation to make use of a burial ground, and in those days superstition, if nothing else, would mitigate against its use.

Mrs. Fradgley informs me that a year or two ago, when drainage work was being carried out, another human skeleton, or part of one, was dug up: unfortunately no inquest was held on this, and the men who unearthed it buried it again before reporting it, and did not mark the spot. The finding of this skeleton seems to lend support to the possibility of the existence of a burial ground, but personally I am inclined to think that they were isolated burials, such as were not uncommon in the middle ages, and even later, when tramps who died by the roadside were often buried where they fell, and indeed such isolated burials are not entirely unknown even now, for it is only a few years ago that a gipsy lad, shot by accident, was buried in the middle of Martlesham Common in Suffolk.

Somewhere about ninety years ago the College gave the land on which our schools are built, and a few years ago Mr. Hinks found a small leaden figure, which had probably belonged to the nuns. Unfortunately it was not taken to the Museum, and has been lost again.

A lady living in Sunningdale has another interesting relic, which may have belonged either to the nunnery, or more probably to the monks at Chertsey. It is a small earthenware pot, glazed inside, and probably used as an inkpot. It has a small handle by which it could be hung on to a belt. This pot was probably made in the twelfth or beginning of the thirteenth century, and was found on Chobham Common.

Comparatively little of the land belonging to the nunnery now remains attached to Broomhall Farm. Broomhall Waste, which was locally known as Starveall Farm, a name which graphically described the poverty of its land, has been built on; all the Station Hill, which for many years was only partially cultivated, has been converted into golf links, and has become a residential district; Titlark's Hill is covered with modern houses; villas have been built by the side of the London Road, and the remaining parts are being gradually absorbed.

CHAPTER VII

PORTNALL PARK, WENTWORTH, AND THE LONDON ROAD

ALTHOUGH Portnall Park is not in the parish of Sunningdale, it has for several centuries been so intimately connected with us that I make no apology for including it here.

Until the beginning of the nineteenth century Portnall, as it is now known (although the original name was "Potnall") included most of what we know as "Wentworth", and was a place of very considerable extent.

Our brook, which was at one time a very much more considerable stream than it is now, in its course from Sunningdale to the Thames at Chertsey, was joined by several other brooks, two or three of them uniting in the low, swampy ground at Blacknest, and from there forming a large stream, later known as "Virginia River," and now Virginia Water. This river meandered through the swamps, which have now been drained into Virginia Water, to a point somewhere near the waterfall of the present day, and near that part was a small hamlet gathered round a mill, known as "Harpesford." All trace of this village has now disappeared, although I believe that some years ago a few tiles which were supposed to have belonged to it were found, but I have been unable to trace what became of them, or indeed who it was that discovered them - probably they were found when Virginia Water was being extended, between 1790 and 1823, after the bursting of the dam in the storm of 1768.

Harpesford seems to have been a Saxon village, for we find it mentioned in the Egham boundaries soon after the Conquest, and Portnall would, from the same document, appear to be the land then known as the "Sire Giffren's Heath de la Croix," but even then the part near Shrubs Hill, later known as "Potnall Warren," bore the name "Poddenhale."

As we have seen in the chapter on Broomhall, the manor of Potnall was for many years owned by the nunnery at Broomhall, by whom it was leased for a long period to two Egham men, who sold it to Edward IV, although they had no power thus to dispose of the property, which up until that time had apparently not been enclosed, for it is described as a "Waste in the Forest of Windsor." It would seem that the nuns made no attempt to interfere in this transaction, for we cannot trace any protest from them until the reign of Henry VIII, when they made an unsuccessful petition to the King for its return. It is quite possible that they regarded the transaction merely as a transfer of the lease, and that this protest was made on the expiration of the term for which they had let it. It seems hardly feasible otherwise that they should have suffered this injustice for very nearly a hundred years without making some move, and then make a belated effort to obtain restitution.

The petition was not granted, but in 1528 Henry handed over Potnall to William Fitzwilliam, who was to pay to the Sheriff of Surrey a red rose each year. Fitzwilliam's nephew, Viscount Montague, succeeded him, and in November, 1566, sold it to Henry Lane.

This Henry Lane was the owner of Coworth Park, and thus Potnall became connected with Sunningdale. In 1574 Lane mortgaged

Potnall, most likely when he purchased the Manor of Sunninghill, which he disposed of in 1583. After the death of his first wife (Ann Norris), he married a wealthy widow, Cicelye Wisdom of Leatherlake, or Leatherhead. By some means Potnall seems to have got into the hands of a London Scrivener. How this happened is not quite clear, but possibly he purchased the mortgage from Kydwell and Brooke and so gained possession. But however this may have been, Lane seems to have come to terms with him in some way, for in 1591 Dormer, the Scrivener, gave him a lease for 10,000 years. Lane, in his will, gave his wife one-third of his goods and an annuity of ten pounds, payable by his son Edward out of Coworth.

Henry Lane died in 1595, and his son Edward did not long survive him, for he appears to have died in 1596. In his will he mentions the instructions left by his father that Potnall should be sold to pay his debts, and left Coworth to his son Henry, with his wife as trustee and guardian.

After the death of Edward his widow married John Osborne, of Coworth, and somehow they managed to retain Potnall, for in 1600 they mortgaged it again.

The Osbornes had two sons, John and Philip, the latter of whom succeeded to Potnall, and in 1661 the Lanes of Coworth granted him a lease for a peppercorn rent (probably a mere form to make the succession clear).

Philip Osborne was succeeded by his daughter Jane, the wife of the Rev. Francis Sayer, of Yattendon. She appears not to have lived at Potnall, but to have let it. She left it to her youngest daughter, Ann, who had married the Master Gunner at Windsor Castle. Ann died in 1711, and Potnall went to her daughter Frances, whose husband was the Rev. Thomas Walker, of Tilehurst. They had two daughters, one or both of whom may have succeeded to Potnall, but it is not clear which was the owner, or whether they possessed it jointly, nor exactly how it came into the possession of Dr. Jebb, the Dean of Derry, who was succeeded by his son David, who, after doing a great deal of work in laying out the grounds, sold the greater part of the estate to Culling Charles Smith, whose wife was Ann Wellesley, a sister of the Duke of Wellington.

Culling Smith called his new estate "Wentworth," and built a mansion on it, which he sold to the Count de Morella, a Field Marshal in the Spanish army, who died in 1877 and was succeeded by his wife, the Countess de Morella, whom many of us remember, as she lived until 1915, and who, until she had attained a great age, was a familiar figure in the hunting field. After her death Wentworth was sold to Messrs. Tarrant, of Byfleet, who made golf links on part of the estate and cut up the remainder into building sites.

Portnall, as it now began to be called, was sold to the Rev. Thomas Bisse, who was succeeded by his son, Colonel Challoner Bisse Challoner, who built the present house. He was a very precise man, who hated to see anything out of place. He would walk about the estate with a chain and padlock, and if he could find a cart, a plough or even a wheelbarrow left in a field, he would put his chain through a wheel and lock it up so that it could not be moved, and the man responsible for leaving it would have to apply to him for the key to unlock it, when he would be severely reprimanded for not putting it in its appointed place. He even went so far as to have rooms labelled with metal plates, showing the use for which they were intended; some of these labels remained until comparatively recently. One of them read "This room is to be used for brushing clothes only. No shoe brushes to be brought in here." Over a large window to the kitchen was another, saying, "All tradesmen to deliver goods at the kitchen window." He was, however, a most considerate employer of labour, and although the wages were not high, men remained with him for years. When he died he left legacies to all his servants, indoor and outdoor, who had been employed for a certain specified period, and I understand expressed a wish that his successor should retain their services, a wish that was faithfully carried out, so that many of them remained until, as quite old men, they were pensioned off.

Colonel Challoner married the second daughter of the Count Jerome De Salis. He died childless in 1872 and left Portnall to his brother-in-law, the Rev. H. J. Fane De Salis, Vicar of Bicester. On taking up his residence at Portnall, he resigned that living, but for a great many years gave help in our church whenever required, and no doubt many of the older residents of Sunningdale will remember his slim, wiry, handsome figure and the fine clear voice in which he read the lessons.

He died in 1915, and was succeeded by his eldest son, Rudolph, who disposed of Portnall Park to the Wentworth Golf Club for a Dormy House Club.

It is rather curious that Wentworth, which was a portion of Portnall, sold off only a little more than a century ago, should now give its name to the whole. I fear that in the course of a few years the names Potnall and Portnall will be completely forgotten.

I cannot find out who made Potnall Warren, but judging from the size of some of the slower growing trees, it must have been at least two hundred or more years ago. Possibly it was one of the unprofitable undertakings of Henry Lane, who appears not to have prospered much in his many activities. It must have been a very large and costly undertaking to throw up the large ridges over such an enormous area, with little prospect of a return on the outlay, for in those days rabbits would fetch only a few pence in the markets. I remember reading a list of the prices paid soon after the accession of Queen Elizabeth for the materials for a banquet in the City of London. A number of rabbits were used, and their price was a fraction under twopence each. Probably the fir trees which now cover the site of this stupendous work have been far more valuable than the rabbits ever were, in spite of the loss through fires which have raged among them from time to time.

When talking of Portnall and Wentworth, one's thoughts naturally turn to our main road, which borders these estates for about a mile and a half - from the corner opposite the Wheatsheaf to Shrubs Hill.

It is rather startling to reflect that from the time of the Roman occupation until a little more than two hundred years ago there were practically no real roads in the kingdom; nothing but bridle tracks and a few wagon tracks across the wastes, whose direction varied according to the condition of the ground, any track being abandoned if the conditions were unfavourable, for another which might prove easier. Norfolk, I believe, was an exception. There they had a system of roads which were at least passable. Charles I so much admired these roads that he suggested that that county should be cut up to provide highways for the rest of the kingdom!

Even in Queen Elizabeth's time wheeled traffic was so rare that in the whole city of London there were only thirty wheeled conveyances. Most of the travelling was done on horseback, and merchandise, unless very heavy, was carried on pack horses, heavy packages going very slowly by great wagons with wheels a foot or more wide, drawn by anything from six to eighteen horses.

The general course of both bridle tracks and wagon tracks were, of course, governed by the fords over the rivers, and in many cases some attempt would be made near these fords to provide something like a bit of decent road, because at those points there could be little or no variation in direction.

Such was the causeway at Egham, which was made by a wool merchant to facilitate the conveyance of his wool from Berkshire to London.

Many of us have noticed the sudden change in the direction of our road at the top of Wheatsheaf Hill. The road in a general way follows pretty closely the old straight course of the Roman Road, but as it was originally constructed made a very wide curve, taking it round towards Thorpe Green and thence to Windlesham, thus avoiding the formidable hills now known as the Cut Hills; but in the early part of the eighteenth century the powder mills of Hounslow grew of such great importance owing to the French wars that it was necessary to make a more direct route both to convey timber from the forests for charcoal burning, and to carry the powder to the seaports in the south, so the road was diverted into its present track, following the course of an old bridle way which led past the nunnery at Broomhall, necessitating deep cuttings through the hills above the Wheatsheaf and at Portnall, which had been avoided by the earlier road.

We, who are used to comfortable and safe travelling at high speed, either by road or rail, can with difficulty realise the hardships which our forefathers who were forced to travel had to endure even in the sixteenth and seventeenth centuries, when many arts had already attained a perfection which can hardly be surpassed to-day. Travelling was almost entirely confined to the wealthy, and if for any reason a journey could not be taken on horseback, a great, lumbering, springless, and windowless coach, drawn by four or more horses, would be unearthed, and dragged bumping over hillocks and through morasses at a pace of anything between three and five miles an hour, the monotony being varied by the occasional upsetting of the coach or an encounter with highwaymen. So common were these mishaps that if the journey were of any length, the usual enquiry on arrival at one's destination was "How many times have you been upset?" showing that it was quite an ordinary incident of a journey.

Speaking of a journey undertaken by Prince George of Denmark in December, 1703, part of which was through this district, an attendant says, "We did not get out of our coaches again, save only when we were overturned or stuck in the mud." The last nine miles of their journey were covered in six hours!

Weary and bruised, the travellers would put

up at night at a roadside inn, which might be fairly comfortable and safe, or on the other hand, filthy and unpleasant, with the host quite likely in league with a gang of thieves to whom he would give information concerning his guests, or he might himself pillage their goods, or even murder them for the sake of their possessions. There was such a house on the Bath Road, not a great distance from here, which is still in existence, although needless to say, the old custom has long been discontinued. No wonder our ancestors made their wills before setting out on a journey!

The coming of the roads changed all this, and made travelling much easier, safer, and more rapid, although there were still highwaymen to be dealt with. Roads brought stage-coaches for the conveyance of the mails and the general public, which on favourable stretches of road sometimes attained the remarkable speed of twelve miles an hour! Travelling by coach, although much cheaper than by private carriage, was still expensive, and one may imagine the discomforts of a long journey on the outside in winter time! The charge from the Wheatsheaf to London was 12s. 6d. outside, or inside, £1 1s., and money then was equal to three or four times as much as in the present day. Travelling was therefore out of the question for the majority of the people.

Our road was a very important one, linking up as it did the cities of Salisbury and Winchester and the seaport of Southampton with the metropolis, and, perhaps not quite at first, but later on, was well equipped with a good inn at the end of each mile, and about half way between the inns a roadside pump with a horse trough. One of these pumps was still standing until a few years ago on the grass verge nearly opposite to the entrance to the Church Fields footpath, but the trough had long disappeared. By the beginning of the nineteenth century there was a regular service of seventy-five stage coaches a day, besides a very large number of stage wagons for the conveyance of goods, and a pretty constant stream of foot passengers.

After the introduction of railways the roads fell upon bad times and into comparative disuse for several years. Many of the inns were either pulled down or turned into private residences, such as happened to the old Pelican Inn, a little over a mile from

Sunningdale Station, which, after some alteration, became "Windlesham Cottage"; but many of them remain, and now that the roads have become busier than could have been dreamed possible in the coaching days, are no doubt reaping the reward of their tenacity, and have turned their extensive stables and coach-houses into garages to meet the altered conditions of the twentieth century. One wonders what changes they may have to undergo when the private aeroplane becomes as popular as the car is to-day!

CHAPTER VIII

OUR CHURCH

ON the face of it there would seem not to be much connection between a military camp in the reign of George I and the building of a church a mile and a half away from it in the reign of Victoria, yet I think that the formation of the camp at King's Beeches (then Blackwick Hill) may have been a not unimportant factor in the erection of our church.

The formation of the camp necessitated the construction of a road for communication, and consequently the large gravel pit on Sunningdale Common was vigorously worked. Near by were market gardens, and it is likely, though there is no direct evidence to show that it was so, that the demand for vegetables for the troops may have had some effect on the sales of produce. Anyhow, the population began to grow, and by the time that Queen Victoria came to the throne had reached about six hundred. The nearest church was the one at Sunninghill, and the inhabitants began to think that it was time that we had one of our own, as the parish church at Old Windsor was some six or seven miles away. In 1839 the gravel pit had become quite exhausted, and Mr. Plant, a squatter living near, purchased an acre of it from the parish authorities of Old Windsor, and gave it to the parish for the site of a church, the conveyance being completed on July 8th, 1840. Apparently in the meantime the building had been proceeded with and the church was nearly completed, for it was consecrated on October 22nd of the same year. The following description is given by the Rev. J. G. Cornish, who was vicar here for sixteen years.

"The original church which stood on this site was built in the years 1839-1840 under the title of 'The District Church of Old Windsor' to supply the needs of the people residing in outlying portions of the large parishes of Egham, Chobham, Windlesham, Sunninghill, and Old Windsor. The memorial stone, the sole remaining relic of that date, may be seen under the west window. The inscription on it states that it was laid by Her Royal Highness Princess Augusta on September 27th in the third year of Queen Victoria's reign, and that the architect was Robert Ebbles. The cost of the church was £1,600.

"It was, to judge from an old woodcut, a very plain building, without a chancel, but provided with galleries which gave additional seating accommodation. The site was given by Mr. John Plant, who it seems had purchased the exhausted gravel pit from the surveyors of Old Windsor for this purpose. Shortly after this the district was formed into an Ecclesiastical Parish, the first incumbent being the Rev. J. S. Hird, a tablet to whose memory will be seen in the north chapel. In 1857 the Rev. W. C. Raffles Flint became Vicar of Sunningdale, and in 1860 he resolved to add a chancel and chapel to the church as a memorial to his near relatives, Sir Stamford and Lady Raffles. At the same time the galleries were removed from the nave. An inscription on the north wall of the chancel records the names of the donor and his relations. Some of the old choir seats are now placed in the north chapel, the fabric of which and the chancel remain practically as they were built in 1860.

"The architect under whom this work was carried out was Mr. G. Street. The reredos, which is of this date, contains some beautiful marbles and fine agates, arranged according to the fashion of that time.

"When the original church was erected the population of the district of Sunningdale was about 600, but it increased so rapidly that notwithstanding the alterations made in 1860 the accommodation was soon found to be insufficient, and in the year 1887 the rebuilding of the nave as a memorial of the jubilee of Queen Victoria was resolved on. The design was entrusted to Mr. G. Oldrid Scott, and the work was completed, largely through the generous assistance of Sir William Farmer of Coworth Park. The memorial stone, which was laid on June 13th, 1887, by H.R.H. the Prince of Wales (King Edward VII), may be seen at the west end above that of the original church. The builders were Messrs. J. Norris & Sons of Sunningdale, and the excellence of the workmanship is evident proof that the building of the parish church by parishioners can be carried out now just as it was often done in the middle ages. The wrought iron hinges of the doors are worth noting, and the carving of the screen. This screen is a memorial to the late vicar, the Rev. W. C. Raffles Flint.

"Soon after the chancel was built a small organ was given by Mr. Arbuthnot of Coworth Park, and not long after the nave was rebuilt this was replaced by a much larger one by Willis and a chamber was provided for it by the vicar, the Rev. J. A. Cree. This last involved the loss of the vestry, so the north chapel was used as such until 1905, when the present vestry was added, and in 1907 an altar and marble pavement for the sanctuary having been given by Mr. Trotter, of King's Beeches, the chapel was available for weekday services.

"The choir stalls are a memorial, as the brass above them testifies, 'To the faithful work of the Rev. John Adams Cree, for 19 years Vicar of Sunningdale.'

"The lectern was given in memory of Miss Farrant of Pineacre.

"The cost of the screen to the chapel, in which there is some interesting woodwork, was met by a bequest from Mrs. Lane. The fretwork, though apparently fragile, is strengthened by the method of cutting through three sections of oak, with the grain of the wood arranged transversely.

"Stained Glass Windows. The southern light of the N.W. window contains the glass which was placed in the old church in memory of Samuel Wilberforce, Bishop of Winchester, and formerly Bishop of Oxford, and the Parish Magazine of that time states that the subscriptions varied from a penny to three guineas. The list of subscribers there given is a long one.

"The west window and the central window in the north aisle are in memory of the late Mrs. Hay of Harewood Lodge Sunninghill; they are by Clayton & Bell. Mr. Kempe's work is seen in the south aisle, in the window dedicated to the memory of Miss Hardinge. The north-east window given by the Rev. C. Dent is by Messrs. Butler & Baines. The Arbuthnot window in the south transept is one of much beauty, and was executed by the Royal Tapestry Works, and the adjacent one, given by the late vicar, the Rev. J. A. Cree, by Messrs. Burlinson & Gryll. Mr. Finch, for very many years parish clerk, is commemorated in the small window in the south aisle.

"The Churchyard. As the land given for the church and churchyard was the site of a disused gravel pit, the churchyard was originally in very bad condition. 'The peculiarly gravelly nature of our soil is the cause why the turf presents so ragged an appearance on the graves,' says the Parish Magazine in 1874. In that year, through the generosity of Mr. J. Arbuthnot of Coworth Park, the churchyard was returfed and a new era of tidiness commenced.

"The rebuilding of the nave in 1887 greatly damaged the churchyard. Its restoration was undertaken by Col. the Hon. C. R. Hay-Drummond, and under his charge it remained until his decease in 1918. The church collections on Low Sunday are given to this fund.

"Among the monuments will be seen those of three vicars of Sunningdale, The Revs. J. S. Hird, W. C. Raffles Flint and J. A. Cree. On the north side is the grave of Prince Victor Hohenlohe Langenburg, of St. Bruno in this parish. The fine alabaster bas-relief in the nave, near the south door, was erected to his memory. It was executed by his daughter, Countess Feodore Gleichen.

"At the west end is placed a massive oak

table, a memorial to Mrs. Halfpenny.

"Near the south door is the tombstone of Mr. John Plant, who gave the site for the church.

"Vicars of Sunningdale :

"Rev. J. S. Hird, B.A. 1842-1845
"Rev. F. V. Fosbery, M.A. 1845-1857
"Rev. W. C. Raffles Flint, M.A., Trinity College, Cambridge 1857-1884
"Rev. J. A. Cree, B.D., Fellow of Magdalen College, Oxford 1884-1903
"Rev. J. G. Cornish, M.A. Hertford College, Oxford 1903-1919
"Rev. R. W. H. Acworth, MA., Worcester College, Oxford 1919-1932
"Rev. S. J. S. Groves, M.A. 1932."

To this there is little to add, except that in 1847 a vicarage was built, which was occupied by the vicars from that time until Mr. Cornish left in 1919. It had been added to both by Mr. Flint and Mr. Cree, and had become too expensive to keep up on a small stipend, so in 1920 it was disposed of and pulled down. Part of the land was added to the churchyard, and cottages built upon another portion, and the remainder, after the erection of a new vicarage, sold as a garden.

Some of the older inhabitants may remember that when the church was being rebuilt a pretty general desire was expressed that a peal of bells should be put in it, but owing to the precarious nature of the soil, it was thought that the subjection of the tower to the vibration of heavy bells would be unsafe. Sir William Farmer therefore had a set of Harrington's tubular bells sent down for trial, and the result seemed highly satisfactory, but for some reason they were not retained.

CHAPTER IX

OUR SCHOOLS

LONG before the passing of the Education Act of 1870, our churches had felt the necessity of some form of universal education, and had endeavoured in various ways to supply that want. In many parishes the parish clerk had kept a more or less regular night school in the vestry, where he imparted such knowledge as he possessed to the youth of the village, in return for a small fee. As in most cases the worthy clerk's attainments were somewhat circumscribed, the knowledge he imparted was not profound, but often he was a really good penman, could read with fluency, and had some knowledge of arithmetic, and if his pupils remained long enough with him he was able to teach them to write well, if not grammatically, to read books and newspapers, and to deal with simple arithmetical problems.

In villages such as ours where there was no church, there was often a "dame school," where some elderly woman, generally a widow, who had most probably received some education at the hand of one of these parish clerks, would take a dozen or so of children for a few pence a week and teach them what little she could, generally far less than could be learned from a parish clerk, although there were exceptions where the dame schools were quite good.

Then again, in some parishes the vicar or curate would open his house in the evening to all such as wished to attend a school, and in such lucky parishes the young people had the opportunity, if they so wished, of becoming really well educated. Such was the case in the not far distant parish of Eversley, where Canon Kingsley held a very successful night school, and I believe turned out many very profound scholars.

In our own village there were a couple of dame schools, one at Shrubs Hill and the other near Sunningdale Park, both, I believe, fairly good as dame schools went. The one at Shrubs Hill, which appears to have been intended for children of all ages, was kept by Mrs. Camp, and the one in the village, which catered for infants only, by Mrs. Hobbs.

But as soon as the church had been

successfully built it was felt that something more than these schools was needed to deal with the educational requirements of a growing population, so in November, 1840, a meeting was held to consider the possibility of building a school. Until the necessary funds could be raised, Mr. Steuart, who lived at Sunningdale Park, offered the use of a cottage for a master's residence, and another cottage was rented as a school. The services of Mr. Hope were secured as a schoolmaster, and those of Mrs. Otaway to superintend the needlework done by the girls.

In 1841 the St. John's College generously gave a site for the proposed new school, making a proviso in their deed of gift that the teaching should be according to the principles of the Church of England, or in the event of these principles being departed from the land should revert to them. In January, 1842, the tender of Mr. Mills of Egham was accepted, and in May of that year the children were transferred to the new building, which was built at a total cost of £474 14s. 6d., aided by donations from Queen Victoria, the Privy Council, and several Church Education societies. Most of what was then built has since been pulled down to make room for larger and more modern buildings, but the master's house still remains, and is now used as a clinic in which the medical officer periodically examines the children, and an office for the head master.

Ten years later the committee found it necessary to extend the school, and plans and estimates were obtained with the result that in March, 1854, the additional building was completed, the cost amounting to £252 13s. 6d., being met by public subscription.

With the exception of the instructor in needlework, up until May, 1848, there had been no second teacher, but the committee then resolved that "a certain number of the younger children be placed under the instruction of an assistant teacher, at a salary of £10 a year," and Miss Charlotte Howard (afterwards Mrs. Goddard) was appointed to carry out the duties of an infants' teacher, and in 1851 the sewing class was also placed under her instruction. In 1864 Miss Dennis was engaged as infants' mistress, but Miss Howard apparently continued to superintend the needlework until her resignation in 1865, when Miss Dennis took over the instruction in needlework with the help of a monitor. Meanwhile the population was still increasing, and the number of school children had grown so much that further accommodation became necessary, consequently further enlargements were undertaken in 1867, 1869, and 1872.

In September 1868, it was found advisable "that the infant mistress should be relieved from instruction in needlework, so as to devote her whole time to the infants." Miss Smith was appointed to take charge of the sewing class, a duty which she continued to perform until her death in 1878, when she was succeeded by Mrs. Johnson.

In addition to the ordinary instruction, evening classes had at times been held, and in 1868 these were put on a more permanent footing, much to the benefit of the young people in the village.

I wonder how many of us can remember the old school as it was in the seventies of last century. It was a picturesque building, with rather low walls, leaded windows, and a wide roof, the appearance of which was much improved in 1874 by the addition of a bell turret, which acted as a ventilator. The inside was not ceiled, but open to the rafters and boarding of the roof, which were painted cream colour. There was a window opening into it from the landing of the master's house, and Mr. Wyatt, who was master until 1877, would sometimes go into his house during school hours, taking his cane with him. He would look through this window, and if he saw a boy misbehaving would throw the cane at his feet and tell him to hold it until he came down, when the unfortunate youngster would suffer for his fault.

Still the numbers continued to grow, and in 1883 it was found necessary to throw the classroom which the infants had hitherto used into the school, and to build a new infants' school near by, and in 1889 the central part of the old school was pulled down, and the present large room erected. Eleven years later, in 1900, the two class rooms were enlarged, and about the same time the new infants' school was also enlarged.

The building of the new room in 1889, although it provided a very fine large room, destroyed the picturesqueness of the old school, and from a teaching point of view was perhaps not an unmixed blessing, for it necessitated the holding of three classes in the one room, with only curtains to separate them, and when these classes were dealing with different subjects the result was not altogether happy.

The last enlargement, a considerable one, was carried out in 1928. New rooms were added, and a sliding partition put into the large room, new offices built, and also a caretaker's cottage. It was a costly undertaking, carried out entirely by voluntary subscription. At the same time a drainage scheme was carried out, and connection made to the main sewer, and provision made for many years to come, unless there should be an abnormal increase in the population.

The following is a list of the masters and infants' mistresses from the opening of the schools in 1840:-

        Mr. Hope, 1840-1841.
        Mr. Lewing, 1841-1846.
        Mr. J. Wall, 1846-1850.

Mr. Alfred Williams, 1850-1854.
Mr. Robert Tunstall, 1854-1866.
Mr. C. W. Wyatt, 1866-1877
Mr. G. W. Gray, 1877-1914.
Mr. C. H. Hinks, 1914.
Miss Watkins, 1864-1865.
Miss Caroline Dennis, 1865-1867.
Miss Clara Simms, 1867-1869.
Miss Mary Sanders, 1869-1872.
Miss Sarah Champ, 1872-1891.
Miss Wakelin, 1891-1922.
Miss Tuck, 1922-1926.
Miss Flockton, 1926.

Mr. Wyatt left Sunningdale in 1877 for Bournemouth, but soon after reaching that enterprising town, which was then growing rapidly, he gave up his work at the school and joined a firm of estate agents (McEwan, Brown, Wyatt and Co.), who were responsible for the formation of the large suburb of Boscombe, and also for the development of Southbourne. He died as the result of a cycling accident.

Mr. Gray after his retirement was for many years the librarian at the Durning Library, Ascot, where he was well known and greatly esteemed by the habitues of the library.

There was much to be said in favour of the old system of pupil teachers. During their five years' apprenticeship before proceeding to the training colleges they gained, in their youth, the art of teaching, which is more difficult to acquire in later life, and I think our schools turned out many very efficient teachers, who on leaving college were well fitted to take up responsible positions, several of them going straight from college into important headmasterships, with considerable responsibility attached to them. One, after some years' successful service, became private secretary to the head of an important firm of publishers; another, after being head of a large school in a busy town, was for some time master in a large private school, went to Cambridge, where he became successively mathematical tutor, a member of the examining board in mathematics, law lecturer, and finally law examiner. Whether the present system of training teachers is quite as satisfactory as the old remains to be seen, as there has as yet been insufficient time to fully test by results.

CHAPTER X

THE PAROCHIAL CHARITIES

THE mention of parochial charities rouses up in the minds of many of us pictures of ancient churches with numbers of old, sombre-looking boards fixed against the venerable walls, recording how some parishioner, perhaps centuries ago, left bequests to be expended in bread, or in certain sums of money to be distributed among so many poor people, or so many widows on certain days of the year, or for some similar purpose, or how another had given directions for the building of almshouses to provide dwellings for a certain number of old men or old women, frequently with a dole of a few shillings weekly to assist in maintaining them.

Such are the charities of old parishes, and until the coming of the Parish and District Councils Act, these charities were generally administered by the vicar and churchwardens, who, in most cases, consulted the Vestry as to their disposal, and presented their accounts to that body. Whether the change of administration has been beneficial or not is a matter of opinion and probably depends on conditions in particular localities. We in Sunningdale are not in a position to form ideas on the subject, as our separation from Old Windsor practically coincided with the passing of the Act.

Such legacies are seldom left nowadays, not because people are less charitable - a glance at the bequests published in the newspapers will show that enormous sums are left each year for charitable purposes - but because conditions have changed so much. Two or three hundred years ago the population was practically immobile. Few people had interests outside their own parishes, and knew little of what was happening beyond their own immediate locality. They were born, lived out their lives, and brought up their children, and died without moving more than a mile or two from their parish church.

Now people's interests are wider, and it has become more customary to leave money to objects with a much larger scope than one particular parish, and as a consequence, although many old parishes are comparatively rich in local charities, newer ones have very little to administer, although in the case of a division of parishes, such as took place here in 1894, some allotment of the charities is generally made. In such cases it is only reasonable to suppose that the parent parish, naturally regarding the charities as their own property, although amiably disposed to the infant, rather grudgingly hand over a share to be administered by the new parish, while the new district is apt to claim rather more than their fair share.

In our own case we should certainly have been rather less well provided for had it not been for the efforts and persistency of the late Rev. W. W. Sherren, who was minister of the Congregational Church at the time the separation took place.

As it is we have the administration of the following, which have been placed in the hands of a committee consisting of the Rev. S. J. S. Groves, Mr. Oates, and Mr. Wakelin by the Parish Council.

Gossett's Trust for apprenticeship, amounting to about £2 11s. 8d. per annum, which is allowed to accumulate until there is a sufficient sum in hand to pay a premium for a suitable applicant. Several Sunningdale lads have already been started in useful careers by this fund.

The Fuel Allotment amounts to fifteen pounds eight shillings and eight pence a year; the North Town Tithe to six pounds; Stevens's trust to one pound two shillings; Bonnell's to four pounds three shillings and fourpence; Bannister's to five shillings; Reddington's to two pounds; and Lane's (Coworth) to two pounds per annum.

Of these the Lane's Charity is distributed to eight widows at Easter, and the remaining charities are distributed in coal and groceries. Last year there were thirty-eight recipients at Easter and thirty-nine at Christmas, each of whom had cards entitling them to five shillings' worth of coal and two shillings and sixpence worth of groceries. When new recipients are added to the list they are given the choice of tradesmen; afterwards the cards are made out with that tradesman's name upon it.

Perhaps a few words about the origin of

some of these charities may prove of interest.

Mrs. Catherine Gossett, widow of the Rev. Isaac Gossett, D.D., by her will of December, 1830, left £50 to the poor of Old Windsor, £50 to the poor of New Windsor, and £50 to the poor of Datchet. She died in October, 1831, and the £50 together with £5 for two years' interest was paid over by her son in January, 1834. It was allowed to accumulate until 1874 when it was invested to bring in the sum of £5 3s. 4d. per annum, half of which is paid to Sunningdale.

The Fuel Allotment is derived from the proceeds of the sale of land in Sunningdale, together with accumulated rents for the same land, invested in Consols, one half of the income being paid to Sunningdale and the remainder to Old Windsor.

The North Town Tithe Fund was founded by the will of James Weldon, dated June 3rd, 1686, whereby he gave to Robert Lee and three others, their heirs and assigns, all and singular his tenths and tithes called North Towne Tithes in the parish of Cookham, upon trust, after the decease of his mother, to permit the said rents and profits of the said tenths and tithes to be received by the churchwardens and overseers of Old Windsor for the time being, therewith to buy bread for the poor of Old Windsor, to be by them yearly distributed amongst the said poor in such manner and at such times as the said churchwardens and overseers shall think fit.

* * * *

By an order dated 22nd September, 1896, made in the matter of Weldon's Charity, and of the Charities of Bannister, Bonnell, Fuel Allotment, Gossett, Reddington and Stevens, the Charity Commissioners in execution of the provisions of Section 14 of the Local Government Act, 1894, authorised the Parish Council of Old Windsor and the Parish Council of Sunningdale each to appoint not more than three additional Trustees of each of the said charities.

George Stevens, Esq., of Old Windsor Lodge, announced by letter dated 28th January, 1813, a benefaction of £50 from himself to the poor of the parish, the interest to be given in bread to the most necessitous, at the discretion of the Vicar and

Churchwardens. This sum was invested in Consols and one half of the income is paid to Sunningdale and the other half to Old Windsor.

Sophia Jane Maria Beale Bonnell, by will dated 2nd July, 1831, bequeathed unto Old Windsor parish the sum of £10 a year, free from all deductions, for a dinner every Christmas day to as many poor men and women as that sum would provide with roast beef and good plum pudding, and also with bread, vegetables, and strong beer, such dinner to take place at the Fox public house on Old Windsor Green. And she desired that a tablet might be put up in Old Windsor Church, that the above bequest of £10 a year for a comfortable day for the poor might not be forgotten but strictly observed.

In order to provide the said sum, a total of £333 6s. 8d. Consols was purchased in the names of Trustees, who, by deed poll dated 25th August, 1841, declared that they would stand possessed of the said stock upon the trusts contained in the will aforesaid.

The dinner was given until 1865, when, as it gave rise to disorderly proceedings, it was discontinued, and in lieu thereof a distribution was made of beef, pudding, bread, and beer money.

The dividends, amounting to £8 6s. 8d., are now divided between Old Windsor and Sunningdale.

Mr. Bannister gave 20 sixpenny loaves, to be given to poor housekeepers every Easter Monday, and for which his estate is chargeable. The annual sum of ten shillings is paid by the brewers as a charge on the Fox and Punchbowl public house, Old Windsor. One-half of the income is paid to the treasurer of the Sunningdale Charities and is distributed with the other charities.

William Reddington, by will, dated 11th April, 1855, devised all his freehold property in the parish of Old Windsor, upon trust, to pay £13 clear, to be given in ten sixpenny loaves weekly to ten housekeepers of the parishes of Old Windsor, Langley Marsh, Bucks, and Thorp, Surrey, alternately. This bequest is a charge on the estates of Burfield and Elmlea, Old Windsor. The share of income applicable for the parish of Old Windsor is £4. 6s. per annum, of which two pounds is distributed in the parish of Sunningdale.

Mr. Edward Lane, of New Windsor, late of Coworth in Old Windsor, by will, dated 7th May, 1732, charged the great tithes of Coworth with a sum of forty shillings a year, to be paid on Easter Monday to the churchwardens and overseers, to be by them given to the poor. The yearly sum of £2 is received from the agent of the Earl of Derby, who is the owner of Coworth Park estate and is administered by the trustees of the Sunningdale Parochial Charities.

Although not coming strictly under the head of charities, there are two other funds belonging to the parish which have to be applied for specific purposes. One is the sum realised by the sale of the site of the old gravel pit, on part of which the church was built, while the remainder was bought to build the vicarage on. The money realised was invested in a Trustee Savings Bank, and afterwards transferred to the Post Office Savings Bank. The income from this investment may only be used for work done on the highways, and it was allowed to accumulate for some years and the interest was then withdrawn to provide kerbing for our footpaths.

The other sum is one which was left by the late Mr. John Berry Torry of Shrubs Hill Place to the Congregational Church to assist in paying the minister's stipend.

One or two generous gifts such as this, if left for the interest to be applied in assisting to pay the stipend of a curate, would relieve the vicar and churchwardens of much anxiety and trouble in raising funds.

CHAPTER XI

SUNNINGDALE AND THE ROYAL FAMILY

SUNNINGDALE has for centuries been more or less intimately connected with members of the royal family. The nunnery at Broomhall, if not actually founded by royalty, was under their patronage during the whole or the greater part of its existence, and even before that there is little doubt that William the Conqueror and William Rufus would many times have hunted over the wastes which covered the site of the future village. Probably Henry VIII hunted over here many times when he was a young man, as it was only a short distance from here, at Sunninghill Park, that he signed his first proclamation on coming to the throne. James I, who was fond of hawking, in all probability loosed his falcons many times on the Sunningdale and Chobham Commons, and to come to later times of which we have definite records, we still find the intimacy kept up.

The foundation stone of our first church, built in 1839-1840, was laid by Princess

Augusta, who, after the ceremony, was entertained at Whitmore Lodge by Mr. Mangles, and the foundation stone of the present one by King Edward VII, then of course Prince of Wales, in 1887, Queen Victoria's jubilee year.

When he was Prince of Wales it was King Edward VII's custom for many years to take a house for Ascot week somewhere in this neighbourhood - sometimes Coworth, Titness, Harewood, or Sunningdale Park, and when he did so he generally attended Sunningdale Church on the Sunday following the races. He was at Coworth when his grandson, King Edward VIII, was born.

On the Saturday of race week he generally gave a water picnic on Virginia Water, when a number of boats were put on the lake and a merry party assembled, prominent among whom were King George V and his brother, the late Duke of Clarence. This picnic was generally followed by a dance in the Fishing Temple, and it was during this dance in June, 1894, that King Edward VII received the news of the birth of his grandson. A large party was present, and immediately on receipt of the news they assembled outside the ballroom, and King Edward, then of course Prince of Wales, announced the happy event, and the band struck up the National Anthem, followed by "God Bless the Prince of Wales" and other loyal tunes.

Count Gleichen, afterwards Prince Victor of Hohenlohe, a nephew of Queen Victoria, built St. Bruno nearly sixty years ago, and lived there until his death in 1892, and was frequently visited by the Queen, who used to drive over from Windsor. When Prince Victor, Duke of Clarence, and King George were stationed at Aldershot, they spent many weekends at St. Bruno, and used to accompany the family to our church on Sunday mornings.

Prince Victor of Hohenlohe was buried in our churchyard on a bitterly cold day in January, and it was while attending his funeral that the Duke of Clarence caught the cold which, turning to pneumonia, caused his death. One of the choirmen died from the same cause.

I well remember a short time after the death of Prince Hohenlohe an unostentatious carriage and pair driving up to the churchyard gate, and a short, rather stout old lady alighting, and walking down the path, followed by a footman bearing a wreath, which she took from him and placed on the grave. It was then that I realised that the lady was no other than Queen Victoria herself. She stood by the grave for a few minutes, and then went away as quietly as she had come.

Belvedere Fort, although not actually in our parish, is so near that part of the gardens and the cottage on the estate are in Sunningdale.

Its origin is somewhat obscure, but it would seem originally to have been a cottage or small farmhouse, probably of Tudor times, which was converted into an ornamental fortress after the formation of Virginia Water. Quite possibly it may at one time have been connected with Coworth, and it may well be that the original house was the home of the Darenfords, who for so many years lived at Coworth in conjunction with the Lanes, for it seems pretty clear that the Lanes occupied the house at Coworth Farm, but the dwelling of the Darenfords seems to have been completely lost sight of. It is also possible, although I have been unable to trace any evidence to support such a supposition, that the ground now belonging to the Crown on which the Fort is built may have been at one time part of the Coworth estate. One of my reasons for thinking this may have been so is the fact that roads, when possible, were formed on the boundaries of estates, and as the Staines and Wokingham Road branches off from the London Road just below the Wheatsheaf Hotel, it is quite probable that it marked the boundary between the Crown and Coworth lands as they were at that time. Later on, seeing the possibilities of the old farm house, this land may have been acquired by the Crown after the formation of Virginia Water by the Duke of Cumberland, and the house then converted into a fortress overlooking the lake. Most likely it was so converted in the time of George IV, who was very much interested in Virginia Water, and who built the Fishing Temple, which has recently been demolished, and which was in a direct line with the windows of the Fort. Be that as it may, some alterations, or perhaps rebuilding, appear to have been carried out in the time of William IV, for in my youthful days I well remember a man then living at Shrubs Hill telling me that when he started work at a very tender age (about 1832-1834), his first job was to embed the old gun flints, which were brought over from Windsor Castle in bags, in the cement on the walls of Fort Belvedere, "And a mighty cold job it was, too," said the old man.

In her younger days Queen Victoria was a very frequent visitor to the Fort and she often picnicked there, but as time went on her visits became more rare, and for many years I believe she never went there at all.

In my young days it was in charge of a caretaker, Mr. Turner, an old Crimean veteran, who lived there for many years. In fact he and his predecessor, Mr. Tate, were in charge for a total period of eighty-four years. On the Queen's birthday each year he fired a Royal Salute of twenty-one guns, an event of great importance to us as youngsters. The guns were old brass cannon, and had been, I believe, naval guns which had been remounted on iron carriages. If I remember aright there were forty-eight of them, and some had been for a time mounted on an ornamental frigate placed on Virginia Water. Mr. Turner remained at Fort

Belvedere until his death at an advanced age, when, after considerable alteration, Sir Malcolm Murray, Comptroller of the Household to H.R.H. the Duke of Connaught, came into residence, and occupied it for some years.

During the last few years of Sir Malcolm Murray's tenure of the Fort King Edward VIII, then of course Prince of Wales, had taken houses in Sunningdale for the summer months, and had been a frequent visitor to the Sunningdale, Wentworth and Swinley Golf Links, and he finally decided to make Fort Belvedere his permanent residence. He had extensive alterations made, retaining the old outward appearance as much as possible, but rendering the inside modern and comfortable. Queen Mary took a great interest in her son's new residence, and was responsible for much of the renovation, particularly for the decorations, which were most effective.

As soon as he entered into residence, His Royal Highness set to work on improving the gardens and grounds. He had a fine swimming pool constructed, laid out new gardens, and cut down many old shrubs which had become overgrown and had outlived their usefulness. Although assisted by some of the best horticulturists in the country and a very efficient staff of gardeners, he might often be seen working as hard as the best of them in reducing the estate to order, wielding spade, fork, or axe with all the vigour of the most robust labourer he employed. I think that it is not too much to say that many of the happiest hours of his life were spent at the Fort, and that when obliged to be away, he was always longing to be back to get on with the improvements he had planned.

During the short period he was King he retreated there whenever his arduous duties permitted him to do so, and it was there that his deed of abdication was signed. It seems a great pity, and it must have been a hard struggle for him to have had to leave his favourite residence just as it was reaching perfection. Thousands of ornamental and flowering shrubs that he had planted, some of them with his own hands, are only just coming into their prime, and it must have gone to his heart to have to abandon them without having seen them at their best, but perhaps some day he may be able to return and enjoy the fruits of his labour.

During his residence here he took considerable interest in the neighbourhood, and both before and after his accession to the throne patronised sales, etc., promoted for the benefit of local objects such as the church and schools. A few years ago, when he was Prince of Wales, he very kindly read out the Roll of Honour in Sunningdale Church on the occasion of the special Armistice Day service.

Princess Louise, Duchess of Argyll, has lived for many years at Ribsden, in the Parish of Windlesham, only at short distance from Sunningdale Station by the path over the Black Hill. She has on several occasions opened the Annual Pound Day for the London Mothers' Convalescent Home in Sunningdale.

THE AUTHOR, HIS WIFE, AND DAUGHTER (FROM FRONT RIGHT) WITH POST OFFICE STAFF